BLACK SEA

MEDITERRANEAN SEA

Canary Islands

Morocco

Tunisia

Algeria

Libya

Egypt

TROPIC OF CANCER

West Sahara

Mauritania

Mali

Niger

Chad

Sudan

RED SEA

Eritrea

Djibouti

Senegal

Gambia

Guinea Bissau

Guinea

Burkina Faso

NIGER R.

Nigeria

Sierra Leone

Ivory Coast

Ghana

Togo

Benin

Liberia

Cameroon

Central African Rep.

Ethiopia

Somalia

Eq. Guinea

Sao Tomé Principe

Gabon

Congo R.

EQUATOR

CONGO R.

Uganda

Kenya

D.R. Congo

Rwanda

Burundi

Tanzania

Zanzibar

Atlantic Ocean

Angola

Malawi

Zambia

Zambezi R.

Mozambique

Seychelles

Comores

Zimbabwe

Namibia

Botswana

TROPIC OF CAPRICORN

Madagascar

Swaziland

South Africa

Lesotho

Indian Ocean

"You won't use *African Safari Journal* simply to record your trip. This innovative book — part guidebook, part travel journal — is a nifty planning tool as well. *African Safari Journal* combines standard tourist information with maps, languages, and a thorough, illustration-rich description of the mammals, birds and reptiles and trees you're likely to encounter on your trip. An excellent, all-in-one reference!"

Ann H. Waigand
Editor, *The Educated Traveler*

"Previous editions of *African Safari Journal* have been a valuable source of information for our eight trips to Africa. They have provided relevant and useful information before, during, and after traveling; appropriately concise format for carrying on a safari; informative, interesting, handy, valuable, insightful, well written, accurate and unique. Well done, Mark!"

Steve and Phyllis Brady
Wichita, Kansas

"The *African Safari Journal* was our one-volume travel companion. It provided all the required reference material plus lots of space for our travel notes. With the limited luggage requirements of Africa it was ideal."

Ken and Debby Pash
California

"A wealth of information compacted into a single reference makes packing light an easier task. When many charter flights limit bags to 26 pounds this streamlined approach to reference material is appreciated. The maps, including camp locations, help place the safari into geographic perspective."

Lynn Crawford
Wisconsin

"It is fabulous. Don't think anything has been left out that safarians need to know. By reading your journal notes taken on safari you can relive all those magic moments and breathe life into photos you have taken."

Marion and Pat Kraft
Ft. Lauderdale, Florida

"The compact *African Safari Journal* was an exceptional volume to have with us. It offered us extensive references to the life we saw and an easy way to record the sightings, document experiences, and have some basic information. In this edition much of that has been expanded and supplemented with a wealth of new practical information that will assist any traveler in a new environment. All of this is in a format that is very easy to carry. It is a winner!"

Burt and Flo Fink
Encino, California

African

SAFARI JOURNAL

FOURTH EDITION

BY
MARK W. NOLTING

GLOBAL TRAVEL PUBLISHERS, INC.

African Safari Journal
(Fourth Edition, retitled, completely revised and updated)
ISBN 0-939895-08-0
Cover photo credits
    Lion/vehicle   Alison Nolting/Wilderness Safaris
    Elephant/people Wilderness Safaris
    Leopard in tree   Marilyn Ritz
    Rhino/lion   Margot and Lisa Day
Illustrations and drawings by Duncan Butchart
Proofread by Sandy Pearlman
Graphic design by Pearl and Associates, Inc.
Printed by Victor Graphics
Printed in the United States of America

Previous Edition: TRAVEL JOURNAL AFRICA, 3rd Edition
Copyright © 1994 by Mark W. Nolting

Dear Safarier:

Over the past three decades I have had the privilege of exploring Africa on countless safaris. Having spent hours in preparation for each of my earlier safaris, and in the end having to carry with me several heavy resource books on mammals, reptiles, birds and trees as well as maps, phrase books and a diary, the idea of consolidating all this vital information into one book was formed.

Why do so many people wish to go to Africa? Many seek the wonderful wilderness of a still primitive African continent, where wildlife in its natural and exciting environment still abounds. Others seek contact with wild spaces and traditional African cultures, which can have a meaningful effect on the human spirit — stirring and stimulating the senses, relaxing and revitalizing the mind.

Visiting Africa means getting back to basics and feeling the thrill of experiencing something entirely different from the world in which we live.

The main allure of Africa is that you can find adventure there. When you go on safari, you never know what you're going to see or what is going to happen. Every safari is exciting. With the right planning, there's no finer adventure!

There is no better time to venture to Africa than the present. Go now, while Africa can still deliver all that is promised — and more!

Sincerely,

Mark Nolting

About the Author

Mark W. Nolting has explored and researched the African continent for over 25 years and is the author of *Africa's Top Wildlife Countries*, a 612-page travel guide currently in its fifth edition.

About the Illustrator

Duncan Butchart was born in England and has lived in South Africa since 1970. He has traveled and worked in numerous African countries on projects ranging from tour leader and film researcher to promotional campaign advisor and trainer of nature guides. A naturalist with a far-reaching knowledge of African ecosystems, Duncan has authored and edited a host of books, booklets, periodicals and manuals.

His illustrations have appeared in a variety of magazines, books and other publications, including *The Vultures of Africa* and the *"Wild About"* series of regional nature guides.

African Facts at a Glance

Area: 11,635,000 square miles (30,420,000 km^2)

Approximate size: More than three times the size of the United States; larger than Europe, the United States and China combined; the second largest continent, covering 20 percent of the world's land surface

Population: 625,000,000 (approx.)

Largest waterfall: Victoria Falls (the world's largest waterfall by volume), twice the height of Niagara Falls and one-and-a-half times as wide

Longest river: Nile River (world's longest), 4160 miles (6710 km)

Largest crater: Ngorongoro Crater (largest intact caldera/crater in the world), 12 miles (19 km) wide with its rim rising 1200–1600 feet (366–488 m) off its expansive 102-square-mile (264-km^2) floor

Highest mountain: Mt. Kilimanjaro (highest mountain in the world not part of a range), 19,340 feet (5895 m)

Highest mountain range: Ruwenzoris (Mountains of the Moon), 16,794 feet (5109 m)

Largest lake: Lake Victoria (world's third largest), 26,828 square miles (69,485 km^2)

Largest drainage basin: Congo River Basin (world's second largest), 1,476,000 square miles (3,822,840 km^2)

Largest freshwater oasis: Okavango Delta (Botswana), over 6000 square miles (15,000 km^2)

Largest desert: Sahara (world's largest), larger than the continental United States

Largest land mammal: Elephant (world's largest), over 15,000 pounds (6800 kg)

Largest bird: Ostrich (world's largest), over 8 feet (2.5 m) tall

Deepest lake: Lake Tanganyika (world's second deepest), over 4700 feet (1433 m)

Longest lake: Lake Tanganyika (world's longest), 446 miles (714 km)

Longest rift valley: The Great Rift Valley, a 5900-mile (9500-km) gash from the Red Sea to Lake Malawi, with 30 active volcanoes

Most species of fish: Lake Malawi (500 species)

Tallest people: The Dinka of southern Sudan (world's tallest) generally reach on average 71 inches (180 cm)

Shortest people: The pygmies of the Congo (world's shortest) reach only 49 inches (125 cm)

Dedication

This edition is dedicated to all the individuals responsible for the continued success of tourism to the national parks and wildlife reserves of Africa. Without the commitment and efforts of the guides, researchers, camp and lodge staff, tour operators, national park and reserve personnel and rangers, wildlife societies, etc., the safari experience in Africa would not be as it is today. Through their work many species have been saved from extinction and much of Africa's landscape has been left "untouched." It is the contributions of these people along with the much needed revenue generated by safari enthusiasts that continue to preserve the wildlife and their natural habitats.

Contents

Contents (Continued)

Languages

Safari Glossary

Illustrations and Descriptions

Checklists

Mammal Illustrations and Descriptions

Mammal Illustrations and Descriptions

Mammal Spoor (Footprints)

Reptile Illustrations and Descriptions

Bird Illustrations and Descriptions

Bird Illustrations
and Descriptions

Tree Illustrations and Descriptions

Maps

Maps (Continued)

Charts

Getting Ready for Safari

Journal Author Information

Name: _____

Address: _____

_____

Bus. tel.: _____   Passport #:_____

Home tel.: _____   Issuing authority:_____

Fax: _____   Driver's license #:_____

E-mail: _____   Date of issue:_____

Date of birth: _____ Date of expiration:_____

In case of emergency, contact:

Name: _____

Address: _____

_____

Bus. tel.: _____ Home tel.:_____

Fax: _____ E-mail:_____

Relationship: _____

_____

In case of emergency, contact:

Name: _____

Address: _____

_____

Bus. tel.: _____ Home tel.: _____

Fax: _____ E-mail: _____

Relationship: _____

_____

Additional information:

Note: Keep a copy of your credit card numbers and traveler's check records in a safe place.

African
SAFARI JOURNAL

Medical Information

Allergies: _____

_____ Blood type: _____

_____

_____

Medication presently taking: Prescription numbers:

_____   _____

_____   _____

_____   _____

_____ . _____   _____

_____   _____

Personal physician

Name: _____

Address: _____

_____

Tel.: _____ Fax: _____

E-mail: _____

Specialist physician

Name: _____

Address: _____

_____

Tel.: _____ Fax: _____

E-mail: _____

Optometrist

Name: _____

Address: _____

_____

Tel.: _____ Fax: _____

E-mail: _____

Eye prescription O.D. _____

O.S. _____

☐ I wear contact lenses

Additional information:

Travel Insurance

Company: _____
Policy number: _____
Group number: _____
Telephone: _____
(Collect call): _____
Contact: _____
Trip cancellation coverage: _____
Travel delay: _____
Baggage loss coverage: _____
Medical: _____
Emergency medical
transportation/evacuation: _____
Accidental death
and dismemberment: _____

Health Insurance

Company: _____
Policy number: _____
Group number: _____
Telephone: _____
(Collect call): _____
Contact: _____

Health History

_____
_____
_____
_____
_____
_____
_____
_____
_____
_____

Your Travel Agent

Agent: _____

Company: _____

Address: _____

_____

Bus. tel.: _____

Tel. after hours: _____

Fax: _____

E-mail: _____

Contact name: _____

Your Tour Operator

Company: _____ Country: _____

Address: _____

_____

Bus. tel.: _____

Tel. after hours: _____

Fax: _____

E-mail: _____

Your African Ground Operators

Company: _____ Country: _____

Address: _____

_____

Bus. tel.: _____

Tel. after hours: _____

Fax: _____

E-mail: _____

Company: _____ Country: _____

Address: _____

_____

Bus. tel.: _____

Tel. after hours: _____

Fax: _____

E-mail: _____

Your African Ground Operators
(Continued)

Company: _____ Country: _____

Address: _____

_____

Bus. tel.: _____

Tel. after hours: _____

Fax: _____

E-mail: _____

Company: _____ Country: _____

Address: _____

_____

Bus. tel.: _____

Tel. after hours: _____

Fax: _____

E-mail: _____

Company: _____ Country: _____

Address: _____

_____

Bus. tel.: _____

Tel. after hours: _____

Fax: _____

E-mail: _____

Company: _____ Country: _____

Address: _____

_____

Bus. tel.: _____

Tel. after hours: _____

Fax: _____

E-mail: _____

Travel Companions

Name: _____

Address: _____

_____

Bus. tel.: _____ Passport #: _____

Home tel.: _____ Issuing authority: _____

Fax: _____ Driver's license #: _____

E-mail: _____ Date of issue: _____

Date of birth: _____ Date of expiration: _____

Medical
information: _____

_____

_____

Name: _____

Address: _____

_____

Bus. tel.: _____ Passport #: _____

Home tel.: _____ Issuing authority: _____

Fax: _____ Driver's license #: _____

E-mail: _____ Date of issue: _____

Date of birth: _____ Date of expiration: _____

Medical
information: _____

_____

_____

Name: _____

Address: _____

_____

Bus. tel.: _____ Passport #: _____

Home tel.: _____ Issuing authority: _____

Fax: _____ Driver's license #: _____

E-mail: _____ Date of issue: _____

Date of birth: _____ Date of expiration: _____

Medical
information: _____

_____

_____

Travel Companions

Name: _____

Address: _____

_____

Bus. tel.: _____   Passport #:_____

Home tel.: _____   Issuing authority:_____

Fax: _____   Driver's license #:_____

E-mail: _____   Date of issue:_____

Date of birth: _____Date of expiration:_____

Medical
information: _____

_____

_____

Name: _____

Address: _____

_____

Bus. tel.: _____   Passport #:_____

Home tel.: _____   Issuing authority:_____

Fax: _____   Driver's license #:_____

E-mail: _____   Date of issue:_____

Date of birth: _____Date of expiration:_____

Medical
information: _____

_____

_____

Name: _____

Address: _____

_____

Bus. tel.: _____   Passport #:_____

Home tel.: _____   Issuing authority:_____

Fax: _____   Driver's license #:_____

E-mail: _____   Date of issue:_____

Date of birth: _____Date of expiration:_____

Medical
information: _____

_____

_____

African
SAFARI JOURNAL

Important Addresses

Name: _____
Address: _____
_____
Bus. tel.: _____ Home tel.: _____
Fax: _____ E-mail: _____

Name: _____
Address: _____
_____
Bus. tel.: _____ Home tel.: _____
Fax: _____ E-mail: _____

Name: _____
Address: _____
_____
Bus. tel.: _____ Home tel.: _____
Fax: _____ E-mail: _____

Name: _____
Address: _____
_____
Bus. tel.: _____ Home tel.: _____
Fax: _____ E-mail: _____

Name: _____
Address: _____
_____
Bus. tel.: _____ Home tel.: _____
Fax: _____ E-mail: _____

Name: _____
Address: _____
_____
Bus. tel.: _____ Home tel.: _____
Fax: _____ E-mail: _____

Important Addresses

Name: _____

Address: _____

_____

Bus. tel.: _____ Home tel.: _____

Fax: _____ E-mail: _____

Name: _____

Address: _____

_____

Bus. tel.: _____ Home tel.: _____

Fax: _____ E-mail: _____

Name: _____

Address: _____

_____

Bus. tel.: _____ Home tel.: _____

Fax: _____ E-mail: _____

Name: _____

Address: _____

_____

Bus. tel.: _____ Home tel.: _____

Fax: _____ E-mail: _____

Name: _____

Address: _____

_____

Bus. tel.: _____ Home tel.: _____

Fax: _____ E-mail: _____

Name: _____

Address: _____

_____

Bus. tel.: _____ Home tel.: _____

Fax: _____ E-mail: _____

Important Addresses

Name: _____
Address: _____
_____
Bus. tel.: _____ Home tel.: _____
Fax: _____ E-mail: _____

Name: _____
Address: _____
_____
Bus. tel.: _____ Home tel.: _____
Fax: _____ E-mail: _____

Name: _____
Address: _____
_____
Bus. tel.: _____ Home tel.: _____
Fax: _____ E-mail: _____

Name: _____
Address: _____
_____
Bus. tel.: _____ Home tel.: _____
Fax: _____ E-mail: _____

Name: _____
Address: _____
_____
Bus. tel.: _____ Home tel.: _____
Fax: _____ E-mail: _____

Name: _____
Address: _____
_____
Bus. tel.: _____ Home tel.: _____
Fax: _____ E-mail: _____

Important Addresses

Name: _____

Address: _____

_____

Bus. tel.: _____ Home tel.: _____

Fax: _____ E-mail: _____

Name: _____

Address: _____

_____

Bus. tel.: _____ Home tel.: _____

Fax: _____ E-mail: _____

Name: _____

Address: _____

_____

Bus. tel.: _____ Home tel.: _____

Fax: _____ E-mail: _____

Name: _____

Address: _____

_____

Bus. tel.: _____ Home tel.: _____

Fax: _____ E-mail: _____

Name: _____

Address: _____

_____

Bus. tel.: _____ Home tel.: _____

Fax: _____ E-mail: _____

Name: _____

Address: _____

_____

Bus. tel.: _____ Home tel.: _____

Fax: _____ E-mail: _____

Newly Found Friends

Name: _____

Address: _____

_____

Bus. tel.: _____ Home tel.: _____

Fax: _____ E-mail: _____

Name: _____

Address: _____

_____

Bus. tel.: _____ Home tel.: _____

Fax: _____ E-mail: _____

Name: _____

Address: _____

_____

Bus. tel.: _____ Home tel.: _____

Fax: _____ E-mail: _____

Name: _____

Address: _____

_____

Bus. tel.: _____ Home tel.: _____

Fax: _____ E-mail: _____

Name: _____

Address: _____

_____

Bus. tel.: _____ Home tel.: _____

Fax: _____ E-mail: _____

Name: _____

Address: _____

_____

Bus. tel.: _____ Home tel.: _____

Fax: _____ E-mail: _____

Newly Found Friends

Name: _____
Address: _____
_____
Bus. tel.: _____ Home tel.: _____
Fax: _____ E-mail: _____

Name: _____
Address: _____
_____
Bus. tel.: _____ Home tel.: _____
Fax: _____ E-mail: _____

Name: _____
Address: _____
_____
Bus. tel.: _____ Home tel.: _____
Fax: _____ E-mail: _____

Name: _____
Address: _____
_____
Bus. tel.: _____ Home tel.: _____
Fax: _____ E-mail: _____

Name: _____
Address: _____
_____
Bus. tel.: _____ Home tel.: _____
Fax: _____ E-mail: _____

Name: _____
Address: _____
_____
Bus. tel.: _____ Home tel.: _____
Fax: _____ E-mail: _____

Flight Schedule

	Carrier	Flight #/class	Day of week	Date	Depart	
From						
To						
From						
To						
From						
To						
From						
To						
From						
To						
From						
To						
From						
To						
From						
To						
From						
To						
From						
To						
From						
To						
From						
To						

Flight Schedule

Arrive	Reconfirmed	Ticket #s	Reservation #	Seat #s

Important notes: Carry a photocopy of your tickets/passport in a separate area. Verify frequent flyer accounts and special meal requests. Also note that many airlines require reconfirmation of flights.

African
SAFARI JOURNAL

Safari Itinerary

Day: _____ Date: _____
Depart from: _____ Travel to: _____
Transportation: _____
Accommodation: _____
Activities: _____

Day: _____ Date: _____
Depart from: _____ Travel to: _____
Transportation: _____
Accommodation: _____
Activities: _____

Day: _____ Date: _____
Depart from: _____ Travel to: _____
Transportation: _____
Accommodation: _____
Activities: _____

Day: _____ Date: _____
Depart from: _____ Travel to: _____
Transportation: _____
Accommodation: _____
Activities: _____

Day: _____ Date: _____
Depart from: _____ Travel to: _____
Transportation: _____
Accommodation: _____
Activities: _____

Day: _____ Date: _____
Depart from: _____ Travel to: _____
Transportation: _____
Accommodation: _____
Activities: _____

36

Safari Itinerary

Day: _____ Date: _____

Depart from: _____ Travel to: _____

Transportation: _____

Accommodation: _____

Activities: _____

Day: _____ Date: _____

Depart from: _____ Travel to: _____

Transportation: _____

Accommodation: _____

Activities: _____

Day: _____ Date: _____

Depart from: _____ Travel to: _____

Transportation: _____

Accommodation: _____

Activities: _____

Day: _____ Date: _____

Depart from: _____ Travel to: _____

Transportation: _____

Accommodation: _____

Activities: _____

Day: _____ Date: _____

Depart from: _____ Travel to: _____

Transportation: _____

Accommodation: _____

Activities: _____

Day: _____ Date: _____

Depart from: _____ Travel to: _____

Transportation: _____

Accommodation: _____

Activities: _____

Safari Itinerary

Day: _____ Date: _____

Depart from: _____ Travel to: _____

Transportation: _____

Accommodation: _____

Activities: _____

Day: _____ Date: _____

Depart from: _____ Travel to: _____

Transportation: _____

Accommodation: _____

Activities: _____

Day: _____ Date: _____

Depart from: _____ Travel to: _____

Transportation: _____

Accommodation: _____

Activities: _____

Day: _____ Date: _____

Depart from: _____ Travel to: _____

Transportation: _____

Accommodation: _____

Activities: _____

Day: _____ Date: _____

Depart from: _____ Travel to: _____

Transportation: _____

Accommodation: _____

Activities: _____

Day: _____ Date: _____

Depart from: _____ Travel to: _____

Transportation: _____

Accommodation: _____

Activities: _____

Safari Itinerary

Day: _____ Date: _____
Depart from: _____ Travel to: _____
Transportation: _____
Accommodation: _____
Activities: _____

Day: _____ Date: _____
Depart from: _____ Travel to: _____
Transportation: _____
Accommodation: _____
Activities: _____

Day: _____ Date: _____
Depart from: _____ Travel to: _____
Transportation: _____
Accommodation: _____
Activities: _____

Day: _____ Date: _____
Depart from: _____ Travel to: _____
Transportation: _____
Accommodation: _____
Activities: _____

Day: _____ Date: _____
Depart from: _____ Travel to: _____
Transportation: _____
Accommodation: _____
Activities: _____

Day: _____ Date: _____
Depart from: _____ Travel to: _____
Transportation: _____
Accommodation: _____
Activities: _____

Safari Itinerary

Day: _____ Date: _____

Depart from: _____ Travel to: _____

Transportation: _____

Accommodation: _____

Activities: _____

Day: _____ Date: _____

Depart from: _____ Travel to: _____

Transportation: _____

Accommodation: _____

Activities: _____

Day: _____ Date: _____

Depart from: _____ Travel to: _____

Transportation: _____

Accommodation: _____

Activities: _____

Day: _____ Date: _____

Depart from: _____ Travel to: _____

Transportation: _____

Accommodation: _____

Activities: _____

Day: _____ Date: _____

Depart from: _____ Travel to: _____

Transportation: _____

Accommodation: _____

Activities: _____

Day: _____ Date: _____

Depart from: _____ Travel to: _____

Transportation: _____

Accommodation: _____

Activities: _____

Safari Itinerary

Day: _____ Date: _____

Depart from: _____ Travel to: _____

Transportation: _____

Accommodation: _____

Activities: _____

Day: _____ Date: _____

Depart from: _____ Travel to: _____

Transportation: _____

Accommodation: _____

Activities: _____

Day: _____ Date: _____

Depart from: _____ Travel to: _____

Transportation: _____

Accommodation: _____

Activities: _____

Day: _____ Date: _____

Depart from: _____ Travel to: _____

Transportation: _____

Accommodation: _____

Activities: _____

Day: _____ Date: _____

Depart from: _____ Travel to: _____

Transportation: _____

Accommodation: _____

Activities: _____

Day: _____ Date: _____

Depart from: _____ Travel to: _____

Transportation: _____

Accommodation: _____

Activities: _____

Packing Checklist and Luggage Inventory

1. Check the items listed below to be taken with you on your trip. Add additional items in the blank spaces provided. *Use this list as a guide.* In case of baggage loss, assess the value of items lost and file a claim with your baggage-loss insurance company.
2. Safari clothing can be any comfortable cotton clothing and should be neutral in color (tan, brown, khaki, light green). Avoid dark blue and black, as these colors attract tsetse flies. Note that cotton clothing is also much cooler on safari than synthetic fibers.
3. Please note that all clothes washed on safari *will* be ironed, so cotton clothing is preferable. Synthetic clothing may be damaged.
4. Please read your itinerary carefully as you may have a strict baggage weight limit (i.e., 25 or 33 pounds per person), so please pack accordingly.
5. Virtually *all* safari camps and lodges provide daily laundry service and many provide complimentary shampoo and conditioner, so you can travel with much less clothing and toiletries than you might imagine!

WOMEN'S CLOTHING

- [ ] Sandals
- [ ] Walking shoes or lightweight hiking shoes (not white)
- [ ] Wide-brimmed hat
- [ ] Windbreaker
- [ ] Sweater or sweatshirt
- [ ] 3 pr. safari* pants
- [ ] 3 pr. safari* shorts
- [ ] 5 pr. safari/sport socks
- [ ] 3 short-sleeve safari* shirts
- [ ] 3 long-sleeve safari* shirts
- [ ] Swimsuit/cover-up
- [ ] 1 pr. casual slacks or skirt
- [ ] 1 or 2 blouses
- [ ] Belts
- [ ] 5 sets underwear
- [ ] 3 bras

OPTIONAL

- [ ] 1 cocktail dress
- [ ] 1 pr. dress shoes and nylons/panty hose
- [ ] 1 sports bra

MEN'S CLOTHING

- [ ] Sandals
- [ ] Walking shoes or lightweight hiking shoes (not white)
- [ ] Wide-brimmed hat
- [ ] Windbreaker
- [ ] Sweater or sweatshirt
- [ ] 3 pr. safari* pants
- [ ] 3 pr. safari* shorts
- [ ] 5 pr. safari/sports socks
- [ ] 3 short-sleeve safari* shirts
- [ ] 3 long-sleeve safari* shirts
- [ ] Swim trunks
- [ ] 1 pr. casual slacks

* Any comfortable cotton clothing for safari should be neutral in color (tan, brown, light green, khaki).

MEN'S CLOTHING

- [ ] 1 sports shirt
- [ ] 5 sets underwear
- [ ] Belts
- [ ] Large handkerchief

OPTIONAL

- [ ] 1 pr. dress slacks, shoes and dress socks
- [ ] 1 dress shirt/jacket/tie

TOILETRIES AND FIRST AID

- [ ] Anti-malaria pills
- [ ] Vitamins
- [ ] Aspirin/Tylenol/Advil
- [ ] Motion sickness pills
- [ ] Decongestant
- [ ] Throat lozenges
- [ ] Laxative
- [ ] Anti-diarrhea medicine
- [ ] Antacid
- [ ] Antibiotic
- [ ] Cortisone cream
- [ ] Antibiotic ointment
- [ ] Anti-fungal cream or powder
- [ ] Prescription drugs
- [ ] Medical summary from your doctor (if needed)
- [ ] Medical alert bracelet or necklace
- [ ] Band-aids (plasters)
- [ ] Thermometer
- [ ] Insect repellent
- [ ] Sunscreen/sun block
- [ ] Shampoo (small container)
- [ ] Conditioner (small container)
- [ ] Deodorant

- [ ] Toothpaste
- [ ] Toothbrush
- [ ] Hairbrush/comb
- [ ] Razor
- [ ] Q-tips/cotton balls
- [ ] Nail clipper
- [ ] Emery boards
- [ ] Makeup
- [ ] Tweezers

SUNDRIES

- [ ] Passport (with visas, if needed)
- [ ] International Certificates of Vaccination
- [ ] Air tickets/vouchers
- [ ] Money pouch
- [ ] Credit cards
- [ ] Traveler's checks
- [ ] Personal checks
- [ ] Insurance cards
- [ ] Pocket calculator
- [ ] Sunglasses/guard
- [ ] Spare prescription glasses/contacts
- [ ] Copy of prescription
- [ ] Eyeglass case
- [ ] Travel alarm clock
- [ ] Binoculars
- [ ] Small flashlight (torch) and extra batteries
- [ ] Sewing kit
- [ ] Small scissors
- [ ] Tissues (travel packs)
- [ ] Handiwipes (individual)
- [ ] Anti-bacterial soap
- [ ] Laundry soap (for washing delicates)

- ☐ Large zip-lock bags for damp laundry
- ☐ Copy of *Africa's Top Wildlife Countries*
- ☐ Maps
- ☐ Business cards
- ☐ Pens
- ☐ Deck of cards
- ☐ Reading materials
- ☐ Decaffeinated coffee/herbal tea
- ☐ Sugar substitute

CAMERA EQUIPMENT

- ☐ Lenses
- ☐ Film
- ☐ Camera bag
- ☐ Lens cleaning fluid
- ☐ Lens tissue/brush
- ☐ Extra camera batteries
- ☐ Flash
- ☐ Flash batteries

- ☐ Battery charger and adapters
- ☐ Plastic bags for lenses and camera body
- ☐ Beanbag, small tripod or monopod
- ☐ Stick-on labels to label completed rolls of film
- ☐ Extra video camera batteries
- ☐ Video charger
- ☐ Outlet adapters (3-prong square and round plugs)
- ☐ Cigarette lighter charger (optional)

GIFTS & TRADES

- ☐ T-shirts
- ☐ Pens
- ☐ Inexpensive watches
- ☐ Several postcards from your area/state
- ☐ Children's magazines and books

OTHER

- ☐ _____
- ☐ _____
- ☐ _____
- ☐ _____
- ☐ _____
- ☐ _____
- ☐ _____
- ☐ _____
- ☐ _____
- ☐ _____
- ☐ _____

- ☐ _____
- ☐ _____
- ☐ _____
- ☐ _____
- ☐ _____
- ☐ _____
- ☐ _____
- ☐ _____
- ☐ _____
- ☐ _____
- ☐ _____

Shopping List

Item: _____

Best places
to shop for it: _____

_____

_____

_____

_____

Item: _____

Best places
to shop for it: _____

_____

_____

_____

_____

Item: _____

Best places
to shop for it: _____

_____

_____

_____

_____

Item: _____

Best places
to shop for it: _____

_____

_____

_____

_____

Item: _____

Best places
to shop for it: _____

_____

_____

_____

Shopping List

Item: _____

Best places
to shop for it: _____

_____

_____

_____

_____

Item: _____

Best places
to shop for it: _____

_____

_____

_____

_____

Item: _____

Best places
to shop for it: _____

_____

_____

_____

_____

Item: _____

Best places
to shop for it: _____

_____

_____

_____

_____

Item: _____

Best places
to shop for it: _____

_____

_____

_____

_____

Expenditures

Date: _____
Item/Service: _____
_____
Amount: _____

Date: _____
Item/Service: _____
_____
Amount: _____

Date: _____
Item/Service: _____
_____
Amount: _____

Date: _____
Item/Service: _____
_____
Amount: _____

Date: _____
Item/Service: _____
_____
Amount: _____

Date: _____
Item/Service: _____
_____
Amount: _____

Expenditures

Date: _____
Item/Service: _____

_____

Amount: _____

Date: _____
Item/Service: _____

_____

Amount: _____

Date: _____
Item/Service: _____

_____

Amount: _____

Date: _____
Item/Service: _____

_____

Amount: _____

Date: _____
Item/Service: _____

_____

Amount: _____

Date: _____
Item/Service: _____

_____

Amount: _____

Expenditures

Date: _____

Item/Service: _____

_____

Amount: _____

Date: _____

Item/Service: _____

_____

Amount: _____

Date: _____

Item/Service: _____

_____

Amount: _____

Date: _____

Item/Service: _____

_____

Amount: _____

Date: _____

Item/Service: _____

_____

Amount: _____

Date: _____

Item/Service: _____

_____

Amount: _____

Traveler's Checks Record

Check Amount	Serial Number	Date Cashed	Where Cashed	Exchange Rate

Traveler's Checks Record

Check Amount	Serial Number	Date Cashed	Where Cashed	Exchange Rate

Safari Pages

Airport Departure Taxes

Call an airline servicing your destination or the tourist office, embassy or consulate of the country(ies) in question for current international and domestic airport taxes which are not included in your air ticket and must be paid with cash before departure.

International airport departure taxes often must be paid in U.S. dollars or other hard currency, such as British pounds or German marks. Be sure to have the exact amount required — often change will not be given. Domestic airport departure taxes are usually payable in local currency.

At the time of this writing, international airport departure taxes for the countries in this guide are as follows.

AIRPORT DEPARTURE TAXES			
Country	Taxes due	Country	Taxes due
Botswana	*	Namibia	*
Burundi	$20.00	Rwanda	$20.00
Congo	$20.00	Seychelles	$20.00 approx
Egypt	*	South Africa	*
Kenya	*	Swaziland	$3.00
Lesotho	$30.00 approx	Tanzania	$20.00
Madagascar	$20.00	Uganda	*
Malawi	$20.00	Zambia	$20.00
Mauritius	$15.00 approx	Zimbabwe	$20.00
Mozambique	$20.00		

* Incuded in price of air ticket

Domestic departure taxes are usually less than the equivalent of US $5.00 and can generally be paid in local currency or are included in your air ticket.

Banks

Barclays and Standard Chartered Banks are located in most countries.

Banking Hours

Banks are usually open Monday–Friday mornings and early afternoons, sometimes on Saturday mornings and closed on Sundays and holidays. Most hotels, lodges and camps are licensed to exchange foreign currency. Quite often, the best place to exchange money is at the airport upon arrival.

Credit Cards

Major international credit cards are accepted by most top hotels, restaurants, lodges, permanent safari camps and shops. Visa and MasterCard are the most widely accepted. American Express and Diner's Club are also accepted by most hotels and many businesses.

Currencies

The currencies of Namibia, Lesotho and Swaziland are on a par with the South African rand. The South African rand is widely accepted in Lesotho and Swaziland; however, the currencies of Namibia, Lesotho and Swaziland are not accepted in South Africa.

Current rates for many African countries can usually be found in the financial section of large newspapers, in periodicals such as *Newsweek* and on the Internet.

US $100.00 bills are not generally accepted; smaller denominations should be carried.

Botswana (1 pula = 100 thebe)

Burundi (1 Burundi franc = 100 centimes)

Congo (1 zaire = 100 makutas)

Egypt (1 Egypt pound =100 piatre)

Kenya (1 Kenya shilling = 100 cents)

Lesotho (1 loti = 100 licente)

Madagascar (1 ariary = 5 francs)

Malawi (1 kwacha = 100 tambala)

Mauritius (1 Mauritius rupee = 100 cents)

Mozambique (1 metical = 100 centavos)

Namibia (1 Namibian dollar = 100 cents)

Rwanda (1 Rwanda franc = 100 centimes)

Seychelles (1 Seychelles rupee = 100 cents)

South Africa (1 rand = 100 cents)

Swaziland (1 lilangeni = 100 cents)

Tanzania (1 Tanzania shilling = 100 cents)

Uganda (1 Uganda shilling = 100 cents)

Zambia (1 kwacha = 100 ngwee)

Zimbabwe (1 Zimbabwe dollar = 100 cents)

Diplomatic Representatives in Africa

UNITED STATES OF AMERICA

Botswana: Tel: (267 31) 353982/3/4 Fax: (267 31) 356947 E-mail: usembgab@mega.bw
United States Embassy, P.O. Box 90, Gaborone, Botswana

Burundi: Tel: (257) 223454
United States Embassy, B.P. 1720, Ave. du Zaire, Bujumbura, Burundi

Congo: Tel: (243 12) 21532 or 21628 Fax: (243 12) 21534
B.P. 697, Unit 31550, 310 Ave. des Aviateurs, Kinshasa, Congo

Egypt: Tel: (202) 355-7371 Fax: (202) 357-3200 E-mail: cacairo@state.gov Web site: www.usis.egnet.net
American Embassy Cairo, 5 Latin America St., Garden City, Cairo, Egypt

Kenya: Tel: (254 2) 537800 Fax: (254 2) 537810
United States Embassy, (temporary location) Mombasa Highway, Nairobi, Kenya

Lesotho: Tel: (266) 312-666 Fax: (266) 310-116 E-mail: amles@lesoff.co.za
United States Embassy, P.O. Box 333, Maseru 100, Lesotho

Madagascar: Tel: (261-2) 212-57, 200-89, 207-18 Fax: (261-2) 345-39
United States Embassy, 14–16 Rue Raintovo, Antsahavola, B.P. 620, Antananarivo, Madagascar

Malawi: Tel: (265) 783 166 Fax: (265) 782 471
United States Embassy, P.O. Box 30016, Area 40, Plot #24, Lilongwe 3, Malawi

Mauritius: Tel: (230) 208-2342 E-mail: usembass@intnet.mu
United States Embassy, Rogers Bldg., Fourth Floor, John Kennedy St., Port Louis, Mauritius

Mozambique: Tel: (258-1) 49-27-97 Fax: (258-1) 49-01-14
United States Embassy, Avenida Kenneth Kaunda 193, P.O. Box 783, Maputo, Mozambique

Namibia: Tel: (264) 61 22 1601 Fax: (264) 61 22 9792 E-mail: econcomm@hotmail.com Web site: www.com.na./namtour
United States Embassy, Ausplan Bldg., 14 Lossen St., P.O. Box 9890, Private Bag 12029, Ausspannplatz, Windhoek 9000, Namibia

Rwanda: Tel: (250) 205 755601/2/3
United States Embassy, Blvd. de la Révolution, B.P. 28, Kigali, Rwanda

UNITED STATES OF AMERICA (Continued)

Seychelles: Tel: (248) 255 256   Fax: (248) 225 189
E-mail: usoffice@seychelles.net

U.S. Consular Agency, Victoria House, 1st Floor, Room 112, P.O. Box 251, Victoria, Seychelles

South Africa: Tel: (27 12) 342 1048   Fax: (27 12) 342 2299

United States Embassy, P.O. Box 9536, 877 Pretorius St., Pretoria, South Africa

Johannesburg Consulate: Tel: (27 11) 646-6900 Fax: (27 11) 646 6916

11th Floor, Kine Center, Commissioner & Kruis Streets, P.O. Box 2155, Johannesburg, South Africa

Swaziland: Tel: (268) 404-6441/2/3 E-mail: mintour@realnet.co.sz Web site: www.mintour.gov.sz

United States Embassy, Central Bank Bldg., Warner St., P.O. Box 199, Mbabane, Swaziland

Tanzania: Tel: (255 51) 666010/5   Fax: (255 51) 666701
E-mail: usembassy-darl@cats-net.com

United States Embassy, 140 Msese Road, Kinondon District, P.O. Box 9123, Dar es Salaam, Tanzania

Uganda: Tel: (256 41) 259791/2/3/4/5   Fax: (256 41) 259 794
E-mail: ugaembassy@rocketmail.com Web site: www.ugandaweb.com

United States Embassy, P.O. Box 7007, Kampala, Uganda

Zambia: Tel: (260 1) 262 859   Fax: (260 1) 252 225

United States Embassy, Independence & United National Aves., P.O. Box 31617, Lusaka, Zambia

Zimbabwe: Tel: (263 4) 14 794521 Fax: (263 4) 796488

United States Embassy, 172 Herbert Chitep o Ave., P.O. Box 3340, Harare, Zimbabwe

CANADA

Botswana: Tel: (26 731) 304411 Fax: (26 731) 304411

Consulate of Canada, Plot 182, Queens Road, Gaborone, Botswana

Congo: Tel: (243) 884-1276, 12 34 947, 12 34 147 Fax: (243) 884-1277, 880-3434, 12 34 881

Canadian Embassy, 17, Avenue Pumbu, Commune Gombe, Kinshasa, Democratic Republic of Congo

Egypt: Tel: (202) 3543110 Fax: (202) 3563548
E-mail: cairo@dfait-maeci/gc.ca

Canadian High Commission, Arab International Bank Building, 5 Midan El Saraya El Kobra, Garden City, P.O. Box 1667, Cairo, Egypt

Kenya: Tel: (254) 334033 214804 Fax: (254) 226987
E-mail: nrobi@dfait-maeci.gc.ca

CANADA (Continued)

Canadian High Commission, Comcraft House, Haile Selassie Ave., P.O. Box 30481, Nairobi, Kenya

Madagascar: Tel: (261) 2425-59   Fax: (261) 2425-06

Canadian High Commission, c/o Qit-Madascar Minerals Ltd., Villa Paula, Androhibe, Lot 2-J-169 Viall 3H Ivandry, Antananaui ROO 101, Madagascar

Mauritius: Tel: (230) 208-0821   Fax: (230) 208-3391
E-mail: canada@intnet.mu

Canadian High Commission, c/o Blanche Birger Co., Ltd., Port Louis, Mauritius

Mozambique: Tel: (258) 149 2623 Fax: (258) 149 2667

Canadian High Commission, Rue Thomas, Nduda 1345, Maputo, Mozambique

Seychelles: Tel: (255 51) 20651   Fax: (255 51) 46005

Canadian High Commission, 38 Mirambo St., P.O. Box 1022, Dar es Salaam, Tanzania

South Africa: Tel: (27 12) 342 6923   Fax: (27 12) 342 3837
E-mail: pret@dfait-maeci.gc.ca

Canadian High Commission, Private Bag X13, 1103 Arcadia St., Hatfield 0083, Pretoria, South Africa

Johannesburg: Tel: (27 11) 442 3130   Fax: (27 11) 442 3325

E-mail: lilly.rormose@dfaitmaeci.gc.ca

Canadian High Commission, P.O. Box 1394, Parklands, 2121 Johannesburg, South Africa

Tanzania: Tel: (255 51) 112831 Fax: (255 51) 116897
E-mail: canada.hc.dsm@raha.com

Canadian High Commission, 38 Mirambo St., P.O. Box 1022, Dar es Salaam, Tanzania

Uganda: Tel: (256 41) 258141   Fax: (256 41) 234518
E-mail: canada.consulate@infocom.co.ug

Canadian High Commission, IPS building, Parliment Ave., Kampala, Uganda

Zambia: Tel: (260 1) 250 833   Fax: (260 1) 254 176

Canadian High Commission, 5199 United Nations Ave., P.O. Box 31313, Lusaka, Zambia

Zimbabwe: Tel: (263 4) 252181/5 Fax: (263 4) 252186
E-mail: ketiwe.nyanyiwa@dfait-maeci.gc.ca

Canadian High Commission, 45 Baines Ave., P.O. Box 1430, Harare, Zimbabwe

UNITED KINGDOM

Botswana: Tel: (267 31) 352841 Fax: (267) 353768
E-mail: british@bc.bw
British High Commission, Private Bag 0023, Gaborone, Botswana
Burundi: Tel: (257) 223711
British Liaison Office, 43 Ave. Bubanza, B.P. 1344, Bujumbura, Burundi
Permanent staff in Kinshasa, Zaire
Congo: Tel: (243 12) 34775/8 E-mail: ambrit@ic.cd
British High Commission, Avenue des Trois Z, B.P. 8049, Kinshasa, Gombe, Congo
Kenya: Tel: (254 2) 714699 Fax: (254 2) 719486
E-mail: PP&A@Nairobi.mail.fco.gov.uk
British High Commission, Upper Hill Road, P., P.O. Box 30465, Nairobi, Kenya
Lesotho: Tel: (266) 313961 Fax: (266) 310120
E-mail: hcmaseru@lesoff.co.za
British High Commission, P.O. Box MS 521, Maseru 100, Lesotho
Madagascar: Tel: (2612) 20 222 7749 Fax: (26 12) 20 222 6690
E-mail: ukembant@simicro.mg
British High Commission, First Floor, Immeuble "Ny Havana," Cite de 67 Ha, BP 167, Antananarivo, Madagascar
Malawi: Tel: (265) 782400 Fax: (265) 782657
E-mail: britcomm@malawi.net
British High Commission, P.O. Box 30042, Lingadzi House, Lilongwe 3, Malawi
Mauritius: Tel: (230) 211 1361 Fax: (230) 211 1369
E-mail: bhc@bow.intnet.mu
British High Commission, Les Cascades Building, Edith Cavell Street, P.O. Box 1063, Port Louis, Mauritius
Mozambique: Tel: (2581) 420111/2/5/6/7 Fax: (2581) 421666
Av Vladimir I Lenine 310, Caixa Postal 55, Maputo, Mozambique
Namibia: Tel: (264 61) 223022 Fax: (264 61) 228895
British Liaison Office, 116A Lentwein St., P.O. Box 22202, 116 Robert Mugabee Ave., Windhoek, Namibia
Rwanda: Tel: (250) 75219
British High Commission, Honorary Consul, Ave. Paul VI, B.P. 351, Kigali, Rwanda
Permanent staff in Kinshasa, Congo
Seychelles: Tel: (248) 225 356 Fax: (248) 225 127
E-mail: bhcsey@seychelles.net
British High Commission, Oliaji Trade Centre, Francis Rachel Street, P.O. Box 161, Victoria Mahe, Seychelles

UNITED KINGDOM (Continued)

South Africa: Tel: (27 31) 305 2929 20

British Consulate, 19th Floor, The Marine, 22 Gardiner Street, Durban, South Africa 4001 or P.O. Box 1404, Durban 4000 South Africa

Dunkeld Corner, 275 Jan Smuts Av., Dunkeld West 2196, Johannesburg 2001, South Africa

Cape Town: Tel: (27 21) 425 3670 Fax: (27 21) 425 1427

British Consulate General, 15th Floor, Southern Life Centre, 8 Riebeek Street, Cape Town 8001 South Africa

Swaziland: Tel: (268) 404 2581/2/3/4 Fax: (268) 404 2585

British High Commission, 2nd Floor, Gilfillan Street, Private Bag, Mbabane, Swaziland

Tanzania: Tel: (255 51) 117659-64 Fax: (255 51) 112951

British High Commission, Social Security House, Samora Ave., P.O. Box 9200, Dar es Salaam, Tanzania

Uganda: Tel: (256 41) 257054/9 or (256 41) 257301/4

British High Commission, 10-12 Parliament Ave., P.O. Box 7070, Kampala, Uganda

Zambia: Tel: (260 1) 251133 Fax: (260 1) 253798

British High Commission, Independence Ave., P.O. Box 50050, Lusaka, Zambia

Zimbabwe: Tel: (263 4) 793781 or 728716 Fax: (263 4) 728380

British High Commission, Stanley House, Jason Moyo Ave., P.O. Box 4490, Harare, Zimbabwe

Duty-Free Allowances

Contact the nearest tourist office or embassy for current duty-free import allowances for the country(ies) which you intend to visit. The duty-free allowances vary; however, the following may be used as a general guideline: 1–2 liters (approximately 1–2 quarts/33.8–67.4 fluid ounces) of spirits, one carton (200) of cigarettes or 100 cigars.

Electricity

Electric current is 220–240-volt AC 50 Hz.

Adapters: Three-prong square or round plugs are most commonly used.

   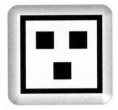

Health

Malarial risk exists in all of Africa's top wildlife countries, so be sure to take your malaria pills (unless advised by your doctor not to take them),as perscribed before, during and after your trip. Contact your doctor, an immunologist or the Centers for Disease Control and Prevention in Atlanta (tel. 1-888-232-3228, fax 1-888-232-3299, Web site: www.cdc.gov) for the best prophylaxis for your itinerary. Use an insect repellent. Wear long-sleeve shirts and slacks for further protection, especially at sunset and during the evening.

Bilharzia is a disease that infests most lakes and rivers on the continent. Do not walk barefoot along the shore or wade or swim in a stream, river or lake unless you know for certain it is free of bilharzia. Bilharzia does not exist in salt water.

If you must get in the water, as with canoe or kayak safaris, do not get out of the canoe or kayak where there are reeds in the water. A species of snail is involved in the reproductive cycle of bilharzia; these snails are more often found near reeds and in slow-moving water. By following your guide's instructions, your risk of contracting the disease is extremely small. If you feel you may have contracted the disease, go to your doctor for a blood test. If diagnosed in its early stages, it is easily cured.

Wear a hat and bring sunblock to protect yourself from the tropical sun. Drink plenty of fluids and limit alcohol consumption at high altitudes.

For further information, obtain a copy of *Health Information for International Travel* from the U.S. Government Printing Office, Washington, D.C. 20402.

Insurance

Travel insurance packages often include a combination of emergency evacuation, medical, baggage, and trip cancellation. We suggest that all travelers to Africa cover themselves fully with an insurance package from a reputable provider. The peace of mind afforded by such insurance far outweighs the cost. Ask your Africa travel specialist for information on relatively inexpensive group-rate insurance.

Metric System of Weights & Measures

The metric system is used in Africa. The U.S. equivalents are listed in the conversion chart below.

MEASUREMENT CONVERSIONS	
1 inch	= 2.54 centimeters (cm)
1 foot	= 0.305 meter (m)
1 mile	= 1.60 kilometers (km)
1 square mile	= 2.59 square kilometers (km^2)
1 quart liquid	= 0.946 liter (l)
1 ounce	= 28 grams (g)
1 pound	= 0.454 kilogram (kg)
1 cm	= 0.39 inch
1 m	= 3.28 feet
1 km	= 0.62 mile
1 km^2	= 0.3861 square mile
1 l	= 1.057 quarts
1 g	= 0.035 ounce
1 kg	= 2.2 pounds

TEMPERATURE CONVERSIONS

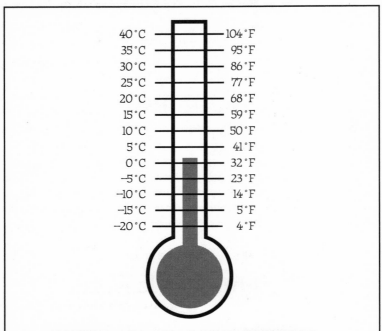

40°C	104°F
35°C	95°F
30°C	86°F
25°C	77°F
20°C	68°F
15°C	59°F
10°C	50°F
5°C	41°F
0°C	32°F
–5°C	23°F
–10°C	14°F
–15°C	5°F
–20°C	4°F

TEMPERATURE CONVERSION FORMULAS

To convert degrees Centigrade into degrees Fahrenheit:
Multiply Centigrade by 1.8 and add 32.

To convert degrees Fahrenheit into degrees Centigrade:
Subtract 32 from Fahrenheit and divide by 1.8.

Money

One way to obtain additional funds is to purchase additional traveler's checks through your American Express or other credit card. Other options include having money sent by telegraph international money order (Western Union), telexed through a bank or sent via international courier (i.e., DHL). Do not count on finding ATM machines, except in South Africa.

Photography Tips

For still wildlife photography, consider bringing an autofocus 35mm camera that can also be adjusted manually, a 35–350mm zoom lens and perhaps a high-quality 1.4 converter. Serious photographers may want to bring along some fixed lenses as well. A 500mm or larger lens is necessary for bird photography. A wide-angle lens (28–35mm) is great for scenic shots. Two camera bodies are preferable, as you can shoot two different speeds of film and have a backup body in case of mechanical failure.

ASA 64 and 100 are best during the day when there is plenty of light. ASA 200–400 is often needed in early mornings and late afternoons, especially when using telephoto or zoom lenses. With very low light, use a flash and/or ASA 1000 or higher film.

For gorilla trekking, a video camera is best for recording your experience. ASA 1000–1600 is recommended for 35mm cameras.

Bring extra camera and flash batteries and plenty of film, as film and batteries may be very expensive and difficult to obtain in parts of Africa. At least 30 rolls of film (per couple) should be packed for a two-week safari.

Digital (still) cameras also work well in the bush; be sure to bring along extra batteries and data cards on which to store the images.

Digital recorders and camcorders are especially useful in low light conditions (i.e., at dawn or dusk or in dense forest). Be sure to bring plug adapters (three-prong square and round adapters), at least three extra batteries, a charging unit and a converter (Africa uses 220–240 volts). Also bring a cigarette lighter charger. Batteries can usually be recharged at your lodge or permanent camp while the generator is running or from your vehicle while you are being driven around.

Bring a beanbag on which to steady your camera. If weight is a problem, then bring the beanbag without the beans and fill it with sand, rice, etc. when you arrive at your destination.

Also consider bringing a small tripod to help steady your camera when shooting from the roof of your roof-hatch vehicle. Monopods (one-legged supports) are also useful, especially on walking safaris and when traveling in open vehicles.

Vehicle vibrations can cause blurry photos, so ask your guide to turn off the engine for those special shots. Protect lenses with UV filters. A polarizer helps cut glare and is especially effective when you have lots of sky and water in the photo. Store cameras and lenses in plastic bags to protect them from dust and humidity, and clean them regularly with lens paper or a lens brush.

Do *not* take photographs of airports, bridges, railway stations, government buildings, telecommunication installations and offices, or military and police installations and personnel. If you do, your camera may be confiscated and you may waste a lot of time explaining why you were taking the photos in the first place.

Safari Tips

Read the "Safari Glossary" to become familiar with the terminology used in the bush. Once on safari, you will notice that when you ask people what animals they saw on their game drive, they might reply, "Elephant, lion, leopard and oryx," when in fact they saw several members of each species. This use of the singular form when more than one member of a species is seen is common. However, one exception to this rule is saying crocs for crocodile. This form of "safariese" will be used throughout this guide to help separate you from the amateur.

Obtain detailed maps of the countries you intend to visit. This will not only increase your awareness of the geography before and during your safari, but will better enable you to relate the story of your safari to family and friends upon your return.

It is often better to sit quietly at a few water holes than to rush around in an attempt to visit as many locations as possible. Don't just look for large game; there is an abundance of reptiles, amphibians, smaller mammals, birds and insects that are often fascinating to observe. Do not disturb the animals. Remember, we are guests in their world.

Instead of just checking species of animals off your checklist and then moving on, concentrate on observing the behavior of the animals around you. Asking your guide about the animal behavior you are observing will open up a whole new level of exploration for you. Most people who take the time to really look find animal behavior fascinating!

Put your valuables in a safety deposit box at your lodge or hotel or in your camp manager's safe.

Do not call out to a person by signaling with your index finger. This is insulting to most Africans. Instead, use four fingers with your palm facing downward.

Wear colors that blend in with your surroundings (brown, tan, light green or khaki). Do not wear perfume or cologne while viewing game. Wildlife can detect unnatural smells for miles and unnatural colors for hundreds of yards (meters), making close approaches difficult.

Do not wade or swim in rivers, lakes or streams unless you know for certain they are free of crocodiles, hippo and bilharzia (a disease). Fast-moving areas of rivers are often safe, but can still be a bit risky. Bilharzia, fortunately, is not the dreaded disease it once was; if detected early, it can be easily cured.

Do not walk along the banks of rivers near dawn, dusk or at night. Those who do so may inadvertently cut off a hippo's path to its water hole, and the hippo may charge. Hippo are responsible for more human deaths in Africa than any other game animal, most often from this type of encounter.

Malaria is present in almost all the parks and reserves in sub-Saharan Africa. Malarial prophylaxis (pills) should be taken and in the United States must be prescribed by a physician. As malaria-carrying mosquitoes come out at dawn, dusk and night, during this period you should use mosquito repellent and wear long pants, a long-sleeve shirt, shoes (not sandals) and socks.

Wear closed-toed shoes or boots at night and also during the day if venturing out into the bush. Bring a flashlight and always have it with you at night.

Don't venture out of your lodge or camp without your guide, especially at night, dawn or dusk. Remember that wildlife is not confined to the parks and reserves in many countries.

Resist the temptation to jog in national parks, reserves or other areas where wildlife exists. To lion and other carnivores, we are just "meat on the hoof" like any other animal — only much slower and less capable of defending ourselves.

The very few tourists who get hurt on safari are almost always those travelers who ignore the laws of nature and most probably the advice and warnings of their guides. Common sense is the rule.

Shopping

If you like bartering, bring clothing (new denims and T-shirts are great) or pens to trade for souvenirs. This works particularly well at roadside stands and in small villages in East and Central Africa, although the villagers are becoming more discerning in their tastes.

SOME SHOPPING IDEAS

Botswana: Baskets, wood carvings, pottery, tapestries and rugs. There are curio shops in many safari camps, hotels and lodges.
Burundi: Crafts available in numerous shops.
Congo: Wood carvings, malachite, copper goods, semiprecious stones and baskets.
Egypt: Papyrus, woven tapestry, hand-blown perfume bottles, cartouche, spices.
Kenya: Makonde and Akomba ebony wood carvings, soapstone carvings, colorful kangas and kikois (cloth wraps). In Mombasa, Zanzibar chests, gold and silverwork, brasswork, Arab jewelry and antiques.
Lesotho: Basotho woven carpets are known worldwide, tapestry weaving and conical straw hats.
Madagascar: Various handmade crafts.
Malawi: Wood carvings, woven baskets.
Mauritius: Intricately detailed, handmade model sailing ships of camphor or teak, pareos (colorful light cotton wraps), knitwear, textiles, T-shirts and Mauritian dolls.
Mozambique: Various handmade crafts.
Namibia: Semiprecious stones and jewelry, karakul wool products, wood carvings and beadwork.
Seychelles: Coco-de-mer, batik prints, spices for Creole cooking and locally produced jewelry, weaving and basketry.
South Africa: Diamonds, gold, wood carvings, dried flowers and wine.
Swaziland: Beautiful hand-woven tapestries, baskets, earthenware and stoneware, and mouth-blown, handcrafted glass animals and tableware.
Tanzania: Makonde carvings, meerschaum pipes and tanzanite.
Uganda: Wood carvings.

Zambia: Wood carvings, statuettes, semiprecious stones and copper souvenirs.

Zimbabwe: Carvings of wood, stone and Zimbabwe's unique verdite, intricate baskets, ceramicware and crocheted garments.

SHOPPING HOURS

Shops are usually open Monday–Friday from 8:00/9:00 a.m. to 5:00/6:00 p.m. and 9:00 a.m. to 1:00 p.m. on Saturdays. Shops in the coastal cities of Kenya and Tanzania often close midday for siesta. Use the shopping hours given above as a general guideline; exact times may vary within the respective country.

Temperature and Rainfall

The temperature and rainfall charts on the following pages give average high and low temperatures and average rainfall for each month of the year for a number of locations. Keep in mind that these are average temperatures; you should expect variations of at least 7°F (5°C) from the averages listed in the charts. Also keep in mind that at higher altitudes you should expect cooler temperatures. This is why many parks and reserves in Africa can be warm during the day and cool to cold at night. The most common packing mistake safariers make is not bringing enough warm layers of clothing!

AVERAGE MONTHLY TEMPERATURES
MIN/MAX IN FAHRENHEIT

CITY	JAN	FEB	MAR	APR	MAY	JUN	JUL	AUG	SEP	OCT	NOV	DEC
EAST AFRICA												
Dar-Es-Salaam	77/88	76/87	76/89	74/87	72/85	68/85	66/84	66/84	68/84	68/86	73/87	76/88
Dodoma	66/86	66/85	64/84	64/84	62/83	57/82	57/79	57/81	59/85	63/88	64/89	65/88
Kigoma	67/81	68/82	68/82	67/82	68/83	67/82	63/83	65/85	67/86	69/85	68/81	67/80
Nairobi	55/78	56/80	58/78	58/76	56/73	54/70	51/70	52/71	53/76	55/77	56/74	55/75
Mombasa	75/88	76/88	77/89	76/87	75/84	74/83	71/81	71/81	72/83	74/85	75/86	76/87
Kampala	65/84	65/83	64/82	64/81	63/79	63/78	63/78	62/78	63/81	63/82	62/81	62/81
Kabale	49/76	50/76	50/75	51/74	51/73	50/73	48/75	49/75	50/76	51/75	50/73	50/73
Kigali	43/68	48/68	46/68	43/68	41/68	37/68	41/68	39/70	37/70	48/68	37/68	39/68
Bujumbura	66/83	66/83	66/83	66/83	66/83	65/85	64/85	65/87	67/89	68/87	67/83	67/83
SOUTHERN AFRICA												
Harare	61/79	61/79	59/79	56/79	50/75	45/71	45/71	47/75	54/80	58/84	60/82	61/79
Victoria Falls	65/85	64/85	62/85	57/84	49/81	43/76	42/77	47/82	55/89	62/91	64/90	64/86
Hwange	64/85	64/84	62/85	56/83	47/80	42/76	40/76	45/81	54/88	61/90	64/89	64/85
Kariba	71/88	71/88	69/88	65/87	58/84	53/80	52/79	57/84	67/91	74/95	74/93	72/89
Mana Pools	71/89	71/89	70/89	67/88	62/85	57/81	56/81	59/86	66/92	73/97	74/95	72/91
Bulawayo	61/82	61/81	60/80	57/80	50/75	46/70	46/71	49/75	55/82	59/86	61/85	61/83
Maun	66/90	66/88	64/88	57/88	48/82	43/77	43/77	48/82	55/91	64/95	66/93	66/90
Lusaka	63/78	63/79	62/79	59/79	55/78	50/73	49/73	53/77	59/84	64/88	64/85	63/81
S. Luangwa	68/90	68/88	66/90	64/90	66/88	54/86	52/84	54/86	59/95	68/104	72/99	72/91
Windhoek	63/86	63/84	59/81	55/77	48/72	45/68	45/68	46/73	54/79	57/84	61/84	63/88
Swakopmund	54/77	54/73	54/73	59/77	59/77	64/82	59/82	59/82	54/77	54/77	54/77	54/77
Johannesburg	59/79	57/77	55/75	52/72	46/66	41/61	41/61	45/66	48/72	54/75	55/77	57/77
Durban	70/82	70/82	68/82	63/79	55/75	50/73	50/73	54/73	59/73	63/75	64/77	68/81
Cape Town	61/79	59/79	57/77	54/73	50/68	46/64	45/63	45/64	46/66	50/70	55/75	59/77

AVERAGE MONTHLY TEMPERATURES
MIN/MAX IN CENTIGRADE

CITY	JAN	FEB	MAR	APR	MAY	JUN	JUL	AUG	SEP	OCT	NOV	DEC
EAST AFRICA												
Dar-es-Salaam	25/32	25/32	24/32	23/31	22/29	20/29	19/28	19/28	19/28	21/29	23/31	24/31
Dodoma	18/29	18/29	18/28	18/28	16/28	15/27	13/27	14/27	15/29	17/31	18/31	18/31
Kigoma	19/27	20/27	20/27	19/27	19/28	188/29	17/28	18/29	19/30	21/29	20/27	19/26
Nairobi	12/25	13/26	14/25	14/24	13/22	12/21	11/21	11/21	11/24	14/25	13/24	13/24
Mombasa	24/32	24/32	25/32	24/31	23/28	23/28	22/27	22/27	22/28	23/29	24/29	24/30
Kampala	18/28	18/28	18/27	18/26	25/17	26/18	26/18	26/17	27/17	27/17	27/17	27/17
Kabale	9/24	11/24	11/24	11/24	11/23	10/23	9/23	10/23	10/24	11/24	11/24	10/24
Kigali					No Numbers							
Bujumbura	19/28	19/28	19/28	19/28	19/28	18/29	18/29	18/31	19/32	20/31	19/29	19/29
SOUTHERN AFRICA												
Harare	17/27	17/27	15/27	13/27	10/24	8/22	7/22	8/24	12/27	14/29	16/28	16/27
Bulawayo	17/28	17/28	16/27	14/27	10/24	8/22	8/22	10/24	12/28	15/30	16/31	16/29
Victoria Falls	18/29	17/29	17/29	14/29	9/27	5/24	7/27	12/31	16/32	18/32	18/31	18/30
Hwange	18/29	18/29	17/29	14/29	9/27	5/24	7/27	12/31	16/32	18/32	18/32	18/30
Kariba	22/31	21/31	21/31	19/31	15/29	12/27	11/26	14/29	19/33	23/35	24/34	22/32
Mana Pools	22/32	21/32	21/32	20/31	17/29	14/27	13/27	15/30	19/34	23/36	23/35	22/33
Maun	19/32	19/31	18/31	14/31	9/28	6/25	6/25	9/28	13/33	18/35	19/34	19/34
Lusaka	17/26	17/26	17/26	15/26	13/25	10/23	10/23	12/25	15/28	18/31	18/30	18/28
S. Luangwa	20/32	20/31	19/32	18/32	19/31	12/30	11/29	12/30	15/35	20/40	22/37	22/33
Windhoek	17/30	17/29	15/27	13/25	9/22	7/20	7/20	8/23	12/26	14/29	16/29	17/31
Swakopmund	12/25	12/23	12/23	15/25	15/25	18/28	15/28	15/28	12/25	12/25	12/25	12/25
Johannesburg	15/26	14/25	13/24	11/22	8/19	5/16	5/16	7/19	9/22	12/24	13/25	14/25
Durban	21/28	21/28	20/28	17/26	13/24	10/23	10/23	12/23	15/23	17/24	18/25	20/27
Cape Town	16/26	15/26	14/25	12/23	10/20	8/18	7/17	7/18	8/19	10/21	13/24	15/25

AVERAGE MONTHLY RAINFALL IN INCHES

CITY	JAN	FEB	MAR	APR	MAY	JUN	JUL	AUG	SEP	OCT	NOV	DEC
EAST AFRICA												
Dar-es-Salaam	2.6	2.6	5.1	11.4	7.4	1.3	1.2	1.0	1.2	1.6	2.9	3.6
Dodoma	6.0	4.3	5.4	1.9	0.2	0	0	0	0	0.2	0.9	3.6
Kigoma	4.8	5.0	5.9	5.1	1.7	0.2	0.1	0.2	0.7	1.9	5.6	5.3
Nairobi	1.5	2.5	4.9	8.3	6.2	1.8	0.7	0.9	1.3	2.2	4.3	3.4
Mombasa	1.1	0.8	2.4	7.7	12.7	4.7	3.5	2.6	2.6	3.4	3.8	2.4
Kampala	1.8	2.4	5.1	6.9	5.8	2.9	1.8	3.4	3.6	3.8	4.8	3.9
Kabale	2.4	3.8	5.2	4.9	3.6	1.2	0.8	2.4	3.7	3.9	4.4	3.4
Kigali	3.5	3.5	4.1	6.5	4.9	1.0	.3	.8	2.4	3.9	3.9	3.5
Bujumbura	3.7	4.4	4.8	4.9	2.3	0.4	0.3	0.4	1.5	2.5	3.9	4.4
SOUTHERN AFRICA												
Harare	7.7	7.1	4.5	1.2	0.5	0.2	0	0.1	0.3	1.2	3.8	6.4
Bulawayo	5.6	4.4	3.3	0.8	0.4	0.1	0	0	0.2	0.8	3.3	4.9
Victoria Falls	6.6	5	2.8	1.0	0.1	0	0	0	0.7	1.1	2.5	6.8
Hwange	5.7	5.1	2.3	0.8	0.1	0	0	0.1	0.8	2.2	5.0	
Kariba	7.5	6.2	4.4	1.2	0.2	0	0	0	0	0.7	2.9	6.9
Mana Pools	8.7	7.1	4.2	1.0	0.2	0	0	0	0	0.5	2.3	9.1
Maun	4.3	3.2	2.8	1.0	0.3	0.1	0	0	0	1.2	2.0	3.8
Lusaka	9.1	7.6	5.7	0.7	0.2	0	0	0	0	0.4	3.6	5.9
S. Luangwa	7.7	11.3	5.6	3.6	0	0	0	0	0	2.0	4.3	4.3
Windhoek	1.7	2.0	2.2	1.1	0.2	0.1	0.1	0.1	0.1	0.4	0.9	1.0
Swakopmund	0.5	0.5	0.5	0.4	0.4	0.4	0.3	0.4	0.4	0.6	0.6	0.4
Johannesburg	4.5	3.8	2.9	2.5	0.9	0.3	0.3	0.2	0.1	2.7	4.6	4.3
Durban	5.1	4.5	5.3	4.2	2.0	1.2	1.4	1.7	2.4	3.9	4.5	4.6
Cape Town	0.6	0.7	0.7	2.0	3.5	3.3	3.5	3.1	2.0	1.4	0.5	0.6

AVERAGE MONTHLY RAINFALL IN MILLIMETERS

CITY	JAN	FEB	MAR	APR	MAY	JUN	JUL	AUG	SEP	OCT	NOV	DEC
EAST AFRICA												
Dar-es-Salaam	66	66	130	292	188	33	33	26	31	42	74	91
Dodoma	152	110	138	49	5	0	0	0	0	5	24	92
Kigoma	123	128	150	130	44	5	3	5	19	28	143	135
Nairobi	39	65	125	211	158	47	15	24	32	53	110	87
Mombasa	25	19	65	197	320	120	90	65	65	87	98	62
Kampala	47	61	130	175	148	73	45	85	90	96	122	99
Kabale	58	97	130	125	92	28	20	58	98	99	110	87
Kigali	90	90	105	165	125	25	7	20	60	100	100	90
Bujumbura	95	110	121	125	56	11	5	11	37	65	100	115
SOUTHERN AFRICA												
Harare	196	179	118	28	14	3	0	3	5	28	97	163
Bulawayo	143	110	85	19	10	3	0	0	5	20	81	123
Victoria Falls	168	126	70	24	3	1	0	0	2	27	64	174
Hwange	145	129	57	20	3	0	0	0	2	21	56	127
Kariba	192	158	113	30	4	1	1	0	1	18	74	175
Mana Pools	221	181	107	26	4	0	0	0	1	13	59	231
Maun	110	80	70	25	7	3	0	0	0	30	50	95
Lusaka	232	192	144	18	3	0	0	0	0	11	92	150
S. Luangwa	195	287	141	91	0	0	0	0	0	50	108	110
Windhoek	43	53	56	28	5	3	3	3	3	10	23	26
Swakopmund	12	15	12	10	10	10	7	9	11	15	16	11
Johannesburg	112	96	74	61	23	8	8	5	3	69	117	109
Durban	130	114	135	107	54	31	36	43	61	99	114	117
Cape Town	15	18	18	50	90	85	90	80	50	36	13	15

Time Zones

EST = Eastern Standard Time (east coast of the United States)
GMT = Greenwich Mean Time (Greenwich, England)

EST + 3/GMT − 2
Cape Verde

EST + 4/GMT − 1
Guinea-Bissau

EST + 5/GMT
Algeria
Ascension
Burkina-Faso
The Gambia
Ghana
Guinea
Ivory Coast
Liberia
Mali
Mauritania
Morocco
St. Helena
São Tomé & Principe
Senegal
Sierra Leone
Togo
Tristan de Cunha

EST + 6/GMT + 1
Angola
Benin
Cameroon
Central African
    Republic
Chad
Congo
Democratic Republic
    of the Congo
    (western)
Equatorial Guinea
Gabon
Niger
Nigeria
Tunisia

EST + 7/GMT + 2
Botswana
Burundi
Democratic Republic
    of the Congo (eastern)
Egypt
Lesotho
Libya

Malawi
Mozambique
Namibia
Rwanda
South Africa
Sudan
Swaziland
Zambia
Zimbabwe

EST + 8/GMT + 3
Comoros
Djibouti
Eritrea
Ethiopia
Kenya
Madagascar
Somalia
Tanzania
Uganda

EST + 9/GM T + 4
Mauritius
Reunion
Seychelles

Tipping

A 10 percent tip is recommended at restaurants for good service, where a service charge is not included in the bill. For advice on what tips are appropriate for guides, ask the Africa specialist booking your safari.

Visa and Inoculation Requirements

Travelers must obtain visas and have proof that they have received certain inoculations for entry into some African countries.

VISA REQUIREMENTS				INOCULATIONS
Country	**U.S.**	**Canada**	**U.K.**	
Botswana	No	No	No	Yellow fever**
Burundi	Yes	Yes	Yes	Yellow fever, cholera
Congo	Yes	Yes	Yes	Yellow fever, cholera
Egypt	Yes	Yes	Yes	Yellow fever**
Kenya	No	No	No	Yellow fever**
Madagascar	Yes	Yes	Yes	Yellow fever**
Malawi	No	No	No	Yellow fever**
Mozambique	Yes	Yes	Yes	Yellow fever**
Namibia	No	No	No	Yellow fever**
South Africa	No	No	No	Yellow fever**
Tanzania	Yes	Yes	Yes	Yellow fever
Uganda	Yes	Yes	Yes	Yellow fever
Zambia	Yes	No	Yes	Yellow fever**
Zimbabwe***	Yes	No	No	Yellow fever**

Notes:

1. Some optional vaccinations include: (a) hepatitis A, (b) hepatitis B, (c) typhoid, (d) tetanus, (e) meningitis, (f) oral polio.
2. Anti-malaria: It is not mandatory but is strongly urged. Anti-malaria is a tablet, not an inoculation. Malaria exists in all of the countries listed above.
3. Cholera: The cholera vaccination is not a guaranteed inoculation against infection, and most countries do not require a cholera vaccination for direct travel from the United States. Check with your local doctor and with embassies of the respective countries. Some require proof of a cholera vaccination even if you are arriving directly from the United States.
4. Yellow fever**: Only if arriving from infected area (i.e., Nigeria).
5. Zimbabwe***: Visa may be obtained on arrival by paying a visa fee.
6. Complete necessary visa forms and return with *your* **valid passport** *(valid for at least six months after travel dates)* to the embassy or consulate concerned or use a visa service.

Wildlife Habitats

Animals are most often found in and nearby the habitats in which they feed or hunt. These habitats fall roughly into four categories — savannah, desert, wetlands and forest.

Savannah is a very broad term that refers to dry land which can be open grasslands, grasslands dotted with trees, or wooded areas. Grazers (grass-eaters) and carnivores (meat-eaters) adept at hunting in savannah are most easily found here. Some browsers (leaf-eaters) also make the savannah their home.

Deserts have little or no standing water and very sparse vegetation. Many desert animals do not drink at all but derive water only from the plants they eat and the condensation formed on them. Some savannah grazers and carnivores can be found in the desert.

African **forests** are thickly vegetated, often with grasses and shrubs growing to about 10 feet (3 m) in height, shorter trees 20–50 feet (6–15 m) high and a higher canopy reaching to 150 feet (45 m) or more.

It is usually more difficult to spot animals in forests than in the other habitats. Many forest animals such as the elephant are more easily seen in open savannah areas. Forest herbivores (plant-eaters) are browsers, preferring to feed on the leaves of plants and fruits usually found in forests. Carnivores have adapted to a style of hunting by which they can closely approach their prey under cover.

Wetlands consist of lakes, rivers and swamps which often are part of a larger savannah or forest habitat. Many rivers wind through savannah regions, providing a habitat within a habitat. Wetlands are good places to see not only wetland species but also other habitat species that go there to drink.

The animals listed in the **Animals by Habitat** chart that follows are classified according to the habitat where most of their time is spent — their most dominant habitat. The animals are listed in order of size by weight.

The major parks and reserves listed in the **Major Wildlife Areas by Habitat** chart are classified according to their most dominant habitats.

Many of these wildlife areas are composed of more than one habitat. Keep in mind that savannah and forest animals may visit wetland habitats to drink and that many forest animals are more easily seen on the open savannah.

A well-rounded safari includes visits to several types of habitats and parks, giving the visitor an overall picture of wildlife and ecosystems.

Animals by Habitat

The animals listed below are classified according to the habitat where most of their time is spent. The animals are listed in order of size by weight.

SAVANNAH/ SAVANNAH WOODLAND		
GRAZERS	**BROWSERS**	**CARNIVORES**
White rhino	Elephant	Lion
Eland	Giraffe	Hyena
Zebra	Kudu	Leopard
Waterbuck	Nyala	Cheetah
Roan antelope	Bushbuck	African wild dog
Gemsbok (oryx)	Gerenuk	Jackal
Topi	Duiker	Serval
Hartebeest	Dikdik	Bat-eared fox
Wildebeest		Mongoose
Tsessebe		Genet
Warthog		
Reedbuck		
Grant's gazelle		
Impala		
Springbok		
Thomson's gazelle		
Klipspringer		
Steenbok		

FOREST		
PRIMATES	**BROWSERS**	**CARNIVORES**
Gorilla	Elephant	Leopard
Chimpanzee	Nyala	Serval
Colobus monkey	Bongo	Genet
Syke's monkey	Bushbuck	
	Duiker	

WETLANDS	
BROWSERS	**CARNIVORES**
Hippopotamus	Crocodile
Buffalo	Otter
Sitatunga	

DESERTS
See savannah grazers, browsers and carnivores above

Major Wildlife Areas by Habitat

P - Primary Habitat   S - Secondary Habitat   [R] - Riverine [L] - Lake
EAST AND CENTRAL AFRICA

COUNTRY	WILDLIFE AREA	SAVANNAH	FOREST	WETLAND
	Arusha (N.P.)		P	S
Tanzania	Lake Manyara	S		P[L]
	Ngorongoro	P		S[L]
	Serengeti	P		S [R]
	Tarangire	P		S [R]
	Mt. Kilimanjaro		P	
	Selous	P		S [R]
	Ruaha	P		S [R]
	Mikumi	P		
	Gombe Stream		P	S [L]
	Mahale Mountains		P	S [L]
Kenya	Nairobi (N.P.)	P		
	Amboseli	P		S
	Tsavo	P		
	Masai Mara	P		S [R]
	Mt. Elgon		P	
	Aberdere		P	
	Mt. Kenya		P	
	Meru	P	S	
	Lake Naivasha			P [L]
	Lake Nakuru	S		P [L]
	Lake Bogoria			P [L]
	Lake Baringo			P [L]
	Samburu	P		S [R]
	Lewa Downs	P		
Uganda	Murchison Falls	P		S [R]
	Queen Elizabeth N.P.	P		S [L]
	Bwindi		P	
	Kibale		P	
Rwanda	Volcano Nat. Park		P	
Congo	Virunga (Rwindi area)	P		S [L]
	Virunga (other areas)	S	P	
	Kahuzi-Biega		P	

Major Wildlife Areas by Habitat

P - Primary Habitat   S - Secondary Habitat   [R] - Riverine   [L] - Lake

SOUTHERN AFRICA

COUNTRY	WILDLIFE AREA	SAVANNAH WOODLAND	FOREST	WETLAND	DESERT
Zimbabwe	Hwange	P			
	Matusadona	S		P [L]	
	Chizarira	P			
	Mana Pools	S		P [R]	
	Matobo	P			
Botswana	Okavango Delta			P	
	Moremi	P		S	
	Linyanti	S		P	
	Savute	P			
	Chobe	P		S [R]	
	Kalahari Desert	S			P
Zambia lower	North & South Luangwa	P		S [R]	
	Zambezi	S		P [R]	
	Kafue	P		S	
Namibia	Etosha	P			S
	East Caprivi	P		S	
	Damaraland				P
	Namib-Naukluft				P
South Africa	Kruger	P		S [R]	
	Private Reserves (Kruger)	P			
	Kgalagadi Trans-Frontier Park				P
	Hluhluwe Umfolozi	P			

Star Gazing
in the
Southern
Hemisphere

Star Gazing
in the Southern Hemisphere

Breathtaking views of the night sky are a typical feature of clear nights in African wilderness areas.

A cloudless night provides a glorious opportunity to become familiar with several interesting constellations and noteworthy stars, as well as up to five planets. The position of the stars and the constellations is constant, but is determined by the position of our own planet Earth, which, of course, revolves around the Sun, as well as the time of night at which observations are made. So it is that the position of the stars appears different to us at different times of the night and throughout the year. Gazing up at the night sky certainly provides a clear indication of the Earth's mobile state, and an understanding of this was the foundation for the human-invented calendar.

Sophisticated computer programs now make it possible to obtain a precise picture of the night sky, based on one's own position (coordinates) at a particular time. A revolving planisphere (two adjustable polyvinyl chloride wheels) is another reliable way to "read" the sky.

With so many thousands of stars, it is quite impossible for the novice to gain anything but a general picture of the night sky, and most will be happy being able to locate and identify the Southern Cross (or Crux) when it is viewable and other major constellations such as Orion and Scorpio. One or more of the planets Venus, Jupiter or Mars will be visible at any given time.

Planets (like our own) do not emit light, but reflect light from the Sun, around which all nine planets in our solar system revolve. Because of this, planets appear as constant unblinking bright spots. Stars, on the other hand, are sources of light (like our Sun) and appear as flickering bright spots when we view them.

The diagrams on pages 82 and 83 provide a very simplistic picture of the Southern Sky in summer and winter. They are not intended as precise tools, but merely as an indication of what you might look for.

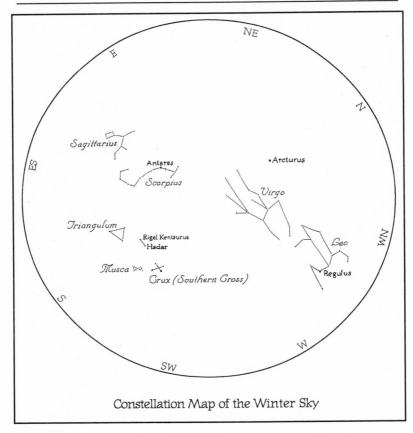

Constellation Map of the Winter Sky

Many guides possess a good knowledge of the night sky and will be able to point out some of the constellations and planets and perhaps even relate interesting fables and stories regarding the origin of their names. If you have more than just a passing interest in skywatching, it would be advisable to bring along your own planisphere or a guidebook, for ready reference.

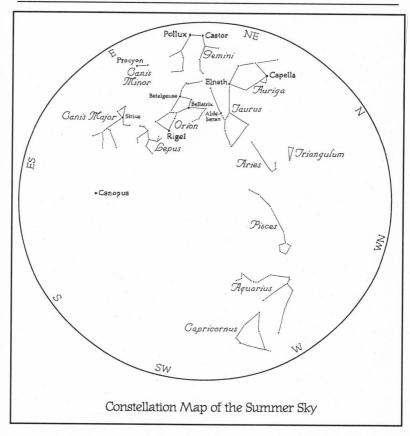

Constellation Map of the Summer Sky

A good pair of binoculars will greatly enhance skywatching, as you'll see up to ten times as many stars! Even seemingly "sparse" parts of the sky will be seen to be filled with hundreds of distant stars when you use binoculars, and a scan of the Milky Way is quite astounding. The Moon itself is magnificent to view through binoculars, as the various craters and so-called "Sea of Tranquillity" become obvious. Because it is so bright, detail on the surface of the Moon is best viewed early in the evening before it is totally dark.

Map
Directory

South, East and Central Africa

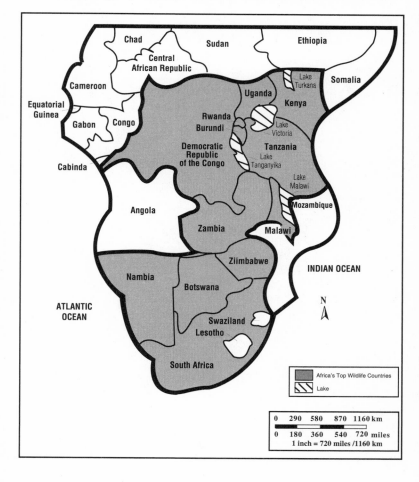

Chad

Sudan

Ethiopia

Central
African Republic

Lake
Turkana

Somalia

Cameroon

Uganda

Kenya

Equatorial
Guinea

Rwanda

Gabon   Congo

Burundi

Lake
Victoria

Democratic
Republic
of the Congo

Tanzania

Cabinda

Lake
Tanganyika

Lake
Malawi

Mozambique

Angola

Zambia

Malawi

INDIAN OCEAN

Ziimbabwe

N

Nambia

Botswana

ATLANTIC
OCEAN

Swaziland

Lesotho

South Africa

Africa's Top Wildlife Countries

Lake

| 0 | 290 | 580 | 870 | 1160 km |

| 0 | 180 | 360 | 540 | 720 miles |

1 inch = 720 miles /1160 km

East and Central Africa

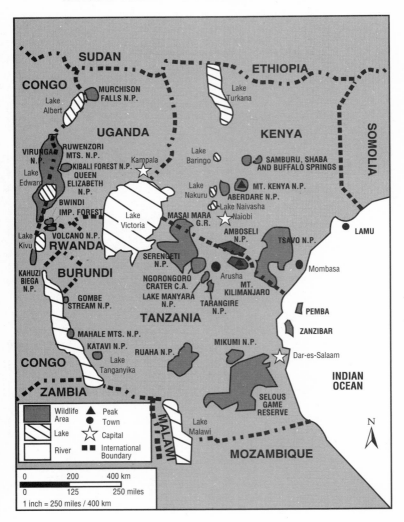

Southern Africa

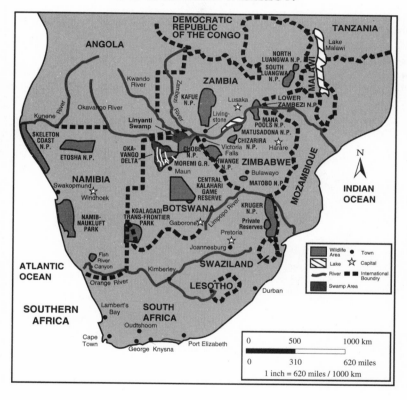

ANGOLA

DEMOCRATIC
REPUBLIC
OF THE CONGO

TANZANIA

Lake
Malawi

NORTH
LUANGWA N.P.

SOUTH
LUANGWA
N.P.

ZAMBIA

Kwando
River

KAFUE
N.P.

Lusaka

Okavango River

Kunene

River

Linyanti
Swamp

Living-
stone

LOWER
ZAMBEZI N.P.

MANA
POOLS N.P.

MATUSADONA N.P.

SKELETON
COAST
N.P.

OKA-
VANGO
DELTA

CHOBE
N.P.

Victoria
Falls

CHIZARIRA

Harare

ETOSHA N.P.

MOREMI G.R.

HWANGE
N.P.

ZIMBABWE

Maun

Bulawayo

NAMIBIA

Swakopmund

Windhoek

CENTRAL
KALAHARI
GAME
RESERVE

MATOBO N.P.

MOZAMBIQUE

N

NAMIB-
NAUKLUFT
PARK

KGALAGADI
TRANS-FRONTIER
PARK

BOTSWANA

Gaborone

Limpopo River

KRUGER
N.P.

Private
Reserves

INDIAN
OCEAN

Pretoria

ATLANTIC
OCEAN

Fish
River
Canyon

Kimberley

Joannesburg

SWAZILAND

Orange River

LESOTHO

Durban

SOUTHERN
AFRICA

Lambert's
Bay

SOUTH
AFRICA

Oudtshoorn

Cape
Town

George Knysna

Port Elizabeth

Wildlife Area		Town
Lake		Capital
River		International Boundry
Swamp Area		

0	500	1000 km
0	310	620 miles
1 inch = 620 miles / 1000 km		

Botswana

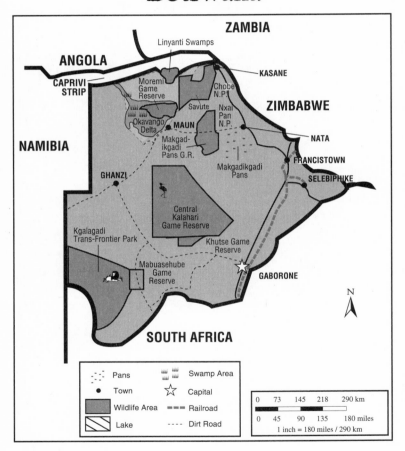

ZAMBIA

Linyanti Swamps

ANGOLA

KASANE

CAPRIVI
STRIP

Moremi
Game
Reserve

Chobe
N.P.

ZIMBABWE

Savute

Nxai
Pan
N.P.

NAMIBIA

Okavango
Delta

MAUN

NATA

Makgad-
ikgadi
Pans G.R.

Makgadikgadi
Pans

FRANCISTOWN

GHANZI

SELEBIPHIKE

Central
Kalahari
Game
Reserve

Kgalagadi
Trans-Frontier Park

Khutse Game
Reserve

Mabuasehube
Game
Reserve

GABORONE

N

SOUTH AFRICA

	Pans		Swamp Area
●	Town	☆	Capital
	Wildlife Area	= = =	Railroad
	Lake	- - - -	Dirt Road

0	73	145	218	290 km
0	45	90	135	180 miles

1 inch = 180 miles / 290 km

Okavango Delta, Moremi Game Reserve and Linyanti Swamp

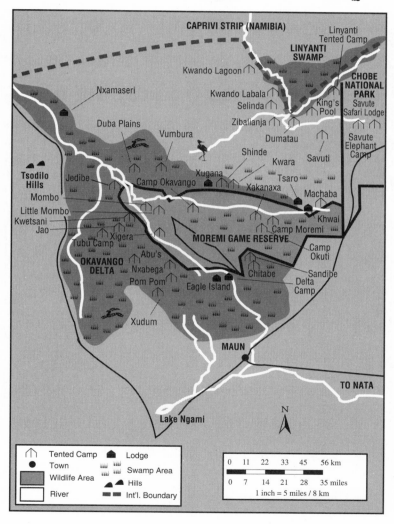

CAPRIVI STRIP (NAMIBIA)

Linyanti
Tented Camp

LINYANTI
SWAMP

Kwando Lagoon

CHOBE
NATIONAL
PARK

Nxamaseri

Kwando Labala

Selinda

King's
Pool

Savute
Safari Lodge

Zibalianja

Duba Plains

Dumatau

Savute
Elephant
Camp

Vumbura

Shinde

Kwara

Savuti

Tsodilo
Hills

Jedibe

Xugana

Tsaro

Camp Okavango

Xakanaxa

Mombo

Machaba

Little Mombo

Khwai

Kwetsani

Jao

Xigera

Camp Moremi

Tubu Camp

MOREMI GAME RESERVE

Abu's

Camp
Okuti

OKAVANGO
DELTA

Nxabega

Pom Pom

Chitabe

Sandibe

Eagle Island

Delta
Camp

Xudum

MAUN

TO NATA

N

Lake Ngami

⌂	Tented Camp	▲	Lodge
●	Town		Swamp Area
	Wildlife Area	▲▲	Hills
	River		Int'l. Boundary

0	11	22	33	45	56 km
0	7	14	21	28	35 miles

1 inch = 5 miles / 8 km

Linyanti Swamp and Savute

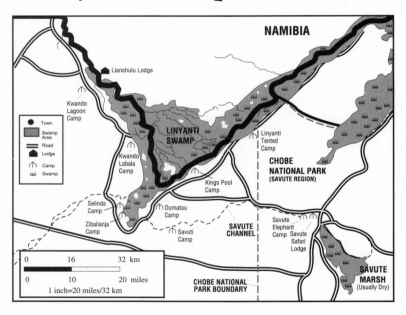

Chobe National Park
(with Savute)

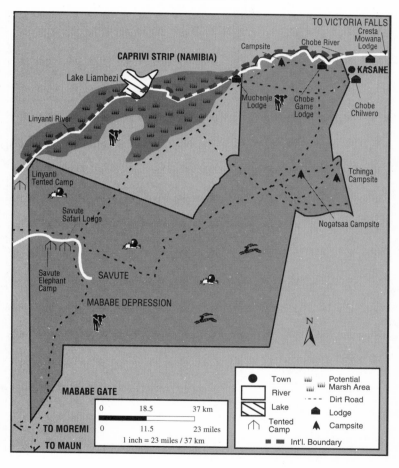

TO VICTORIA FALLS

Cresta Mowana Lodge

CAPRIVI STRIP (NAMIBIA)

Campsite

Chobe River

● KASANE

Lake Liambezi

Muchenje Lodge

Chobe Game Lodge

Chobe Chilwero

Linyanti River

Linyanti Tented Camp

Tchinga Campsite

Savute Safari Lodge

Nogatsaa Campsite

Savute Elephant Camp

SAVUTE

MABABE DEPRESSION

N

MABABE GATE

	Town		Potential Marsh Area
	River	- - -	Dirt Road
	Lake		Lodge
	Tented Camp		Campsite
		■ ■	Int'l. Boundary

0	18.5	37 km
0	11.5	23 miles
1 inch = 23 miles / 37 km		

TO MOREMI

TO MAUN

Burundi

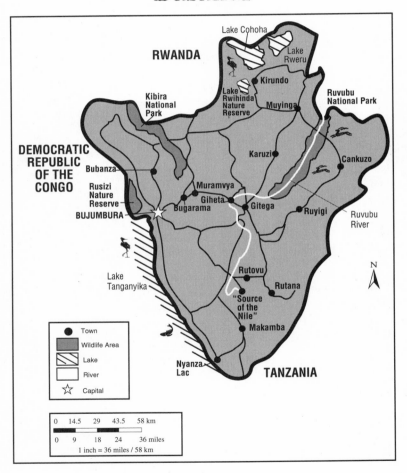

RWANDA

Lake Cohoha

Lake Rweru

Kirundo

Kibira National Park

Lake Rwihinda Nature Reserve

Muyinga

Ruvubu National Park

DEMOCRATIC REPUBLIC OF THE CONGO

Bubanza

Karuzi

Cankuzo

Rusizi Nature Reserve

Muramvya

Giheta

BUJUMBURA

Bugarama

Gitega

Ruyigi

Ruvubu River

Lake Tanganyika

Rutovu

Rutana

"Source of the Nile"

Makamba

● Town

▨ Wildlife Area

◫ Lake

▢ River

☆ Capital

Nyanza Lac

TANZANIA

N

0	14.5	29	43.5	58 km
0	9	18	24	36 miles

1 inch = 36 miles / 58 km

Eastern Democratic Republic of the Congo

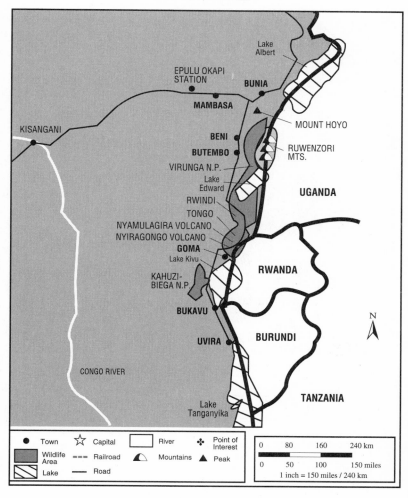

Lake Albert

EPULU OKAPI STATION

BUNIA

MAMBASA

— MOUNT HOYO

KISANGANI

BENI

RUWENZORI MTS.

BUTEMBO

VIRUNGA N.P.

Lake Edward

UGANDA

RWINDI

TONGO

NYAMULAGIRA VOLCANO

NYIRAGONGO VOLCANO

GOMA

Lake Kivu

RWANDA

KAHUZI-BIEGA N.P.

BUKAVU

N

UVIRA

BURUNDI

CONGO RIVER

TANZANIA

Lake Tanganyika

Town	☆ Capital	River	❖ Point of Interest
Wildlife Area	▪▪▪ Railroad	⛰ Mountains	▲ Peak
Lake	— Road		

| 0 | 80 | 160 | 240 km |
| 0 | 50 | 100 | 150 miles |
| 1 inch = 150 miles / 240 km |

Kenya

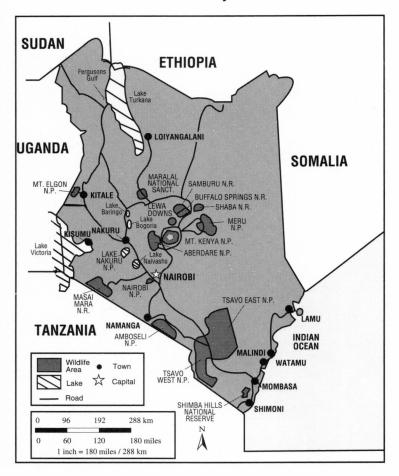

SUDAN

ETHIOPIA

Fergusons Gulf

Lake Turkana

● **LOIYANGALANI**

UGANDA

SOMALIA

MT. ELGON N.P.

MARALAL NATIONAL SANCT.

SAMBURU N.R.

● **KITALE**

BUFFALO SPRINGS N.R.

Lake Baringo

LEWA DOWNS

SHABA N.R.

Lake Bogoria

MERU N.P.

KISUMU **NAKURU**

MT. KENYA N.P.

Lake Victoria

LAKE NAKURU N.P.

Lake Naivasha

ABERDARE N.P.

☆ **NAIROBI**

NAIROBI N.P.

MASAI MARA N.R.

TSAVO EAST N.P.

● **LAMU**

TANZANIA

NAMANGA

AMBOSELI N.P.

INDIAN OCEAN

MALINDI

▨ Wildlife Area	● Town
▨ Lake	☆ Capital
— Road	

TSAVO WEST N.P.

WATAMU

●MOMBASA

0	96	192	288 km
0	60	120	180 miles
1 inch = 180 miles / 288 km			

SHIMBA HILLS NATIONAL RESERVE

SHIMONI

N

Amboseli National Park

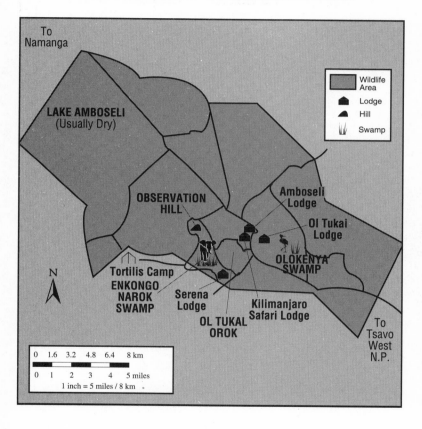

Tsavo National Park

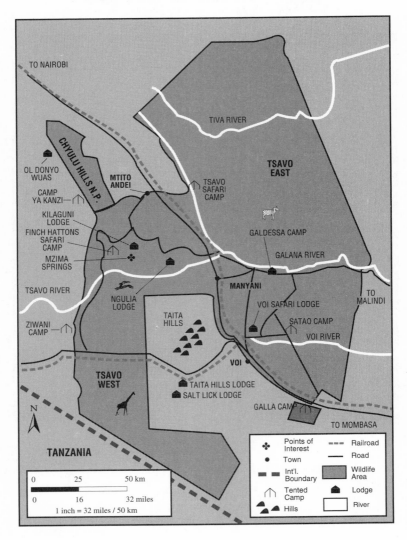

TO NAIROBI

CHYULU HILLS N.P.

TIVA RIVER

TSAVO EAST

OL DONYO WUAS

CAMP YA KANZI

MTITO ANDEI

TSAVO SAFARI CAMP

KILAGUNI LODGE

FINCH HATTONS SAFARI CAMP

MZIMA SPRINGS

GALDESSA CAMP

GALANA RIVER

TSAVO RIVER

NGULIA LODGE

MANYANI

TO MALINDI

ZIWANI CAMP

TAITA HILLS

VOI SAFARI LODGE

SATAO CAMP

VOI RIVER

VOI

TSAVO WEST

TAITA HILLS LODGE

SALT LICK LODGE

GALLA CAMP

TO MOMBASA

N

TANZANIA

Points of Interest	Railroad
Town	Road
Int'l. Boundary	Wildlife Area
Tented Camp	Lodge
Hills	River

0   25   50 km
0   16   32 miles
1 inch = 32 miles / 50 km

Masai Mara National Reserve

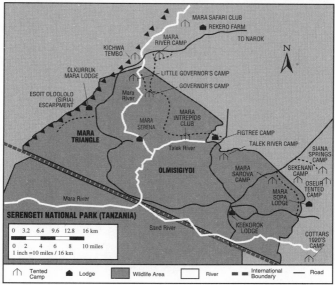

Tented Camp · Lodge · Wildlife Area · River · International Boundary · Road

Samburu, Shaba and Buffalo Springs National Reserves

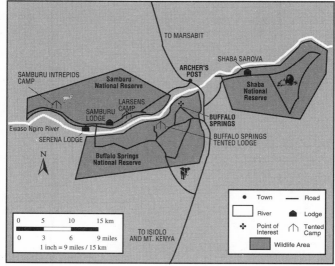

Lesotho

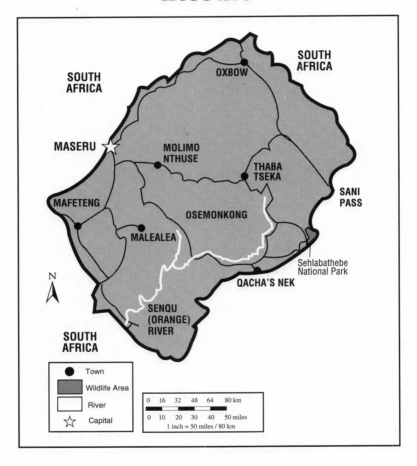

Malawi

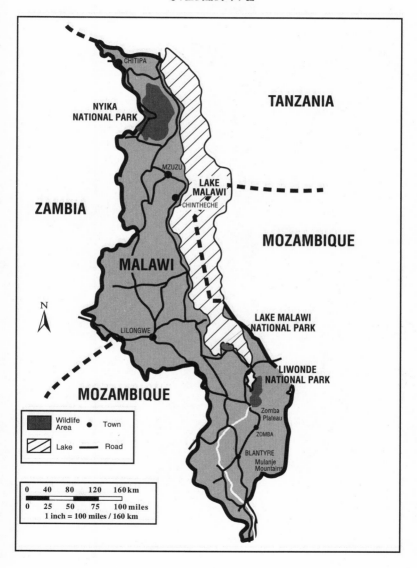

TANZANIA

CHITIPA

NYIKA
NATIONAL PARK

MZUZU

LAKE
MALAWI

CHINTHECHE

ZAMBIA

MOZAMBIQUE

MALAWI

LAKE MALAWI
NATIONAL PARK

LILONGWE

N

LIWONDE
NATIONAL PARK

MOZAMBIQUE

Zomba
Plateau

ZOMBA

BLANTYRE
Mulanje
Mountains

Wildlife Area	● Town
Lake	— Road

0	40	80	120	160 km
0	25	50	75	100 miles

1 inch = 100 miles / 160 km

Liwonde National Park

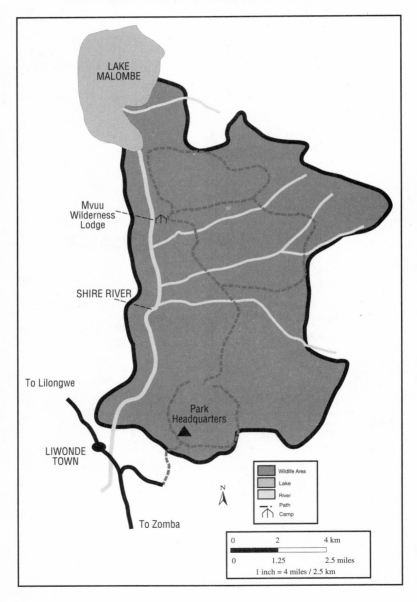

LAKE
MALOMBE

Mvuu
Wilderness
Lodge

SHIRE RIVER

To Lilongwe

LIWONDE
TOWN

Park
Headquarters

To Zomba

N

Wildlife Area
Lake
River
Path
Camp

| 0 | 2 | 4 km |
| 0 | 1.25 | 2.5 miles |

1 inch = 4 miles / 2.5 km

Mauritius

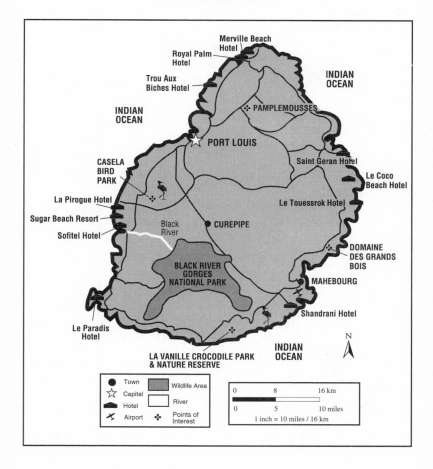

Merville Beach Hotel

Royal Palm Hotel

Trou Aux Biches Hotel

INDIAN OCEAN

INDIAN OCEAN

PAMPLEMOUSSES

PORT LOUIS

CASELA BIRD PARK

Saint Geran Hotel

Le Coco Beach Hotel

La Pirogue Hotel

Le Touessrok Hotel

Sugar Beach Resort

Sofitel Hotel

Black River

CUREPIPE

DOMAINE DES GRANDS BOIS

BLACK RIVER GORGES NATIONAL PARK

MAHEBOURG

Shandrani Hotel

Le Paradis Hotel

N

LA VANILLE CROCODILE PARK & NATURE RESERVE

INDIAN OCEAN

Town	Wildlife Area
Capital	River
Hotel	
Airport	Points of Interest

0	8	16 km
0	5	10 miles
1 inch = 10 miles / 16 km		

Namibia

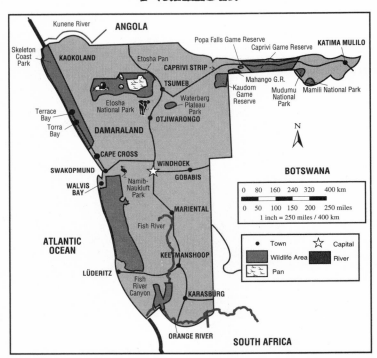

Etosha National Park

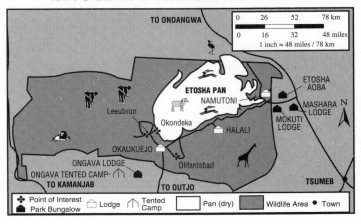

Namib-Naukluft Park

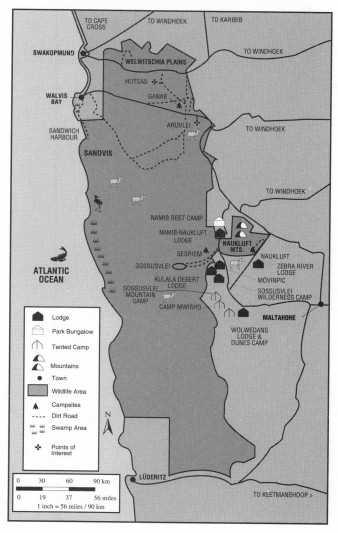

Rwanda

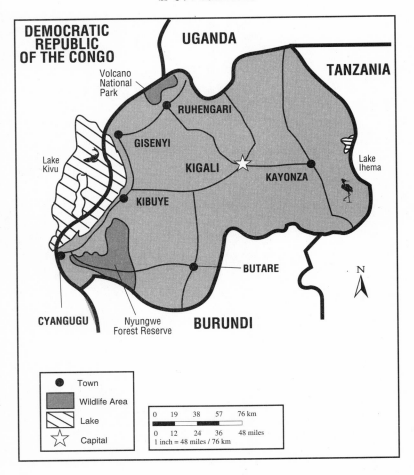

Volcano National Park

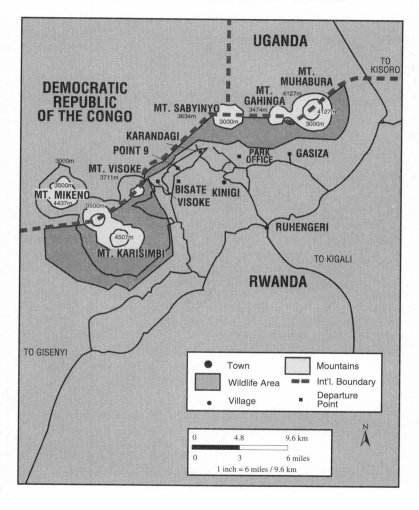

Seychelles

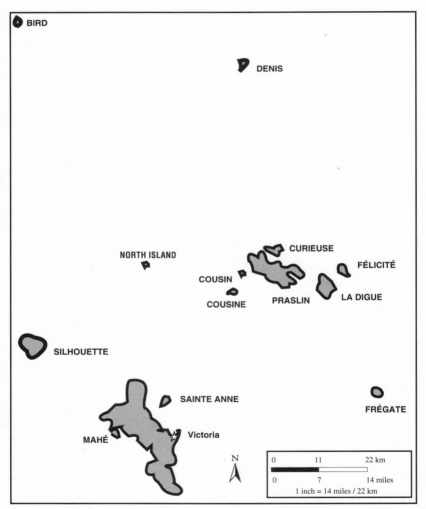

South Africa

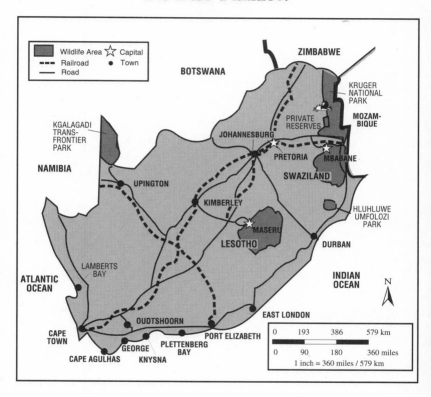

Kruger National Park and Private Reserves

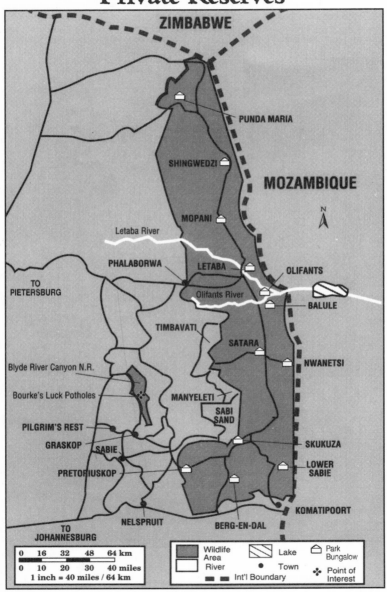

ZIMBABWE

PUNDA MARIA

SHINGWEDZI

MOZAMBIQUE

N

MOPANI

Letaba River

PHALABORWA   LETABA   OLIFANTS

TO
PIETERSBURG   Olifants River

BALULE

TIMBAVATI

SATARA   NWANETSI

Blyde River Canyon N.R.

Bourke's Luck Potholes   MANYELETI

SABI
SAND

PILGRIM'S REST

GRASKOP   SKUKUZA

SABIE

PRETORIUSKOP   LOWER
SABIE

KOMATIPOORT

TO
JOHANNESBURG   NELSPRUIT   BERG-EN-DAL

| 0 | 16 | 32 | 48 | 64 km |

| 0 | 10 | 20 | 30 | 40 miles |

1 inch = 40 miles / 64 km

Wildlife Area — Lake — Park Bungalow
River — Town — Point of Interest
Int'l Boundary

Sabi Sands Game Reserve and Manyeleti Game Reserve

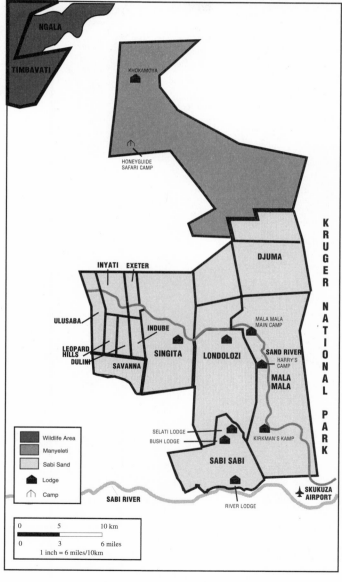

NGALA

TIMBAVATI

KHOKAMOYA

HONEYGUIDE
SAFARI CAMP

K R U G E R   N A T I O N A L   P A R K

DJUMA

INYATI   EXETER

ULUSABA

MALA MALA
MAIN CAMP

INDUBE

LEOPARD
HILLS
DULINI

SINGITA

LONDOLOZI

SAND RIVER

HARRY'S
CAMP

SAVANNA

MALA
MALA

SELATI LODGE

BUSH LODGE

KIRKMAN'S KAMP

Wildlife Area

Manyeleti

Sabi Sand

Lodge

Camp

SABI SABI

SKUKUZA
AIRPORT

SABI RIVER

RIVER LODGE

0	5	10 km
0	3	6 miles

1 inch = 6 miles/10km

Kgalagadi Transfrontier Park

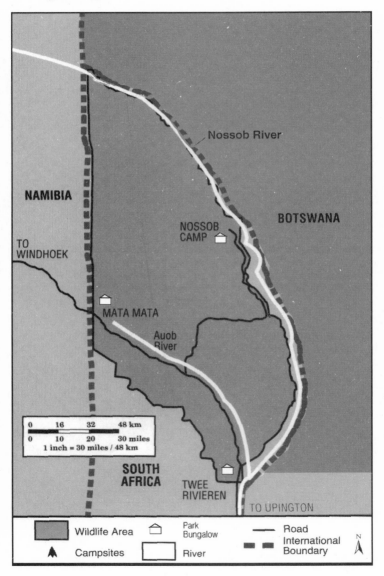

NAMIBIA

TO WINDHOEK

Nossob River

BOTSWANA

NOSSOB CAMP

MATA MATA

Auob River

0	16	32	48 km
0	10	20	30 miles

1 inch = 30 miles / 48 km

SOUTH AFRICA

TWEE RIVIEREN

TO UPINGTON

Wildlife Area   Park Bungalow   Road

Campsites   River   International Boundary

N

Kwa-Zulu Natal Game Reserves

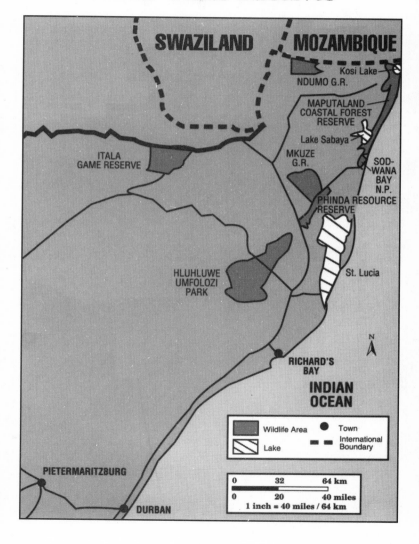

SWAZILAND

MOZAMBIQUE

Kosi Lake

NDUMO G.R.

MAPUTALAND
COASTAL FOREST
RESERVE

Lake Sabaya

ITALA
GAME RESERVE

MKUZE
G.R.

SOD-
WANA
BAY
N.P.

PHINDA RESOURCE
RESERVE

HLUHLUWE
UMFOLOZI
PARK

St. Lucia

N

RICHARD'S
BAY

INDIAN
OCEAN

Wildlife Area   Town

Lake   International
                  Boundary

| 0 | 32 | 64 km |
| 0 | 20 | 40 miles |

1 inch = 40 miles / 64 km

PIETERMARITZBURG

DURBAN

Swaziland

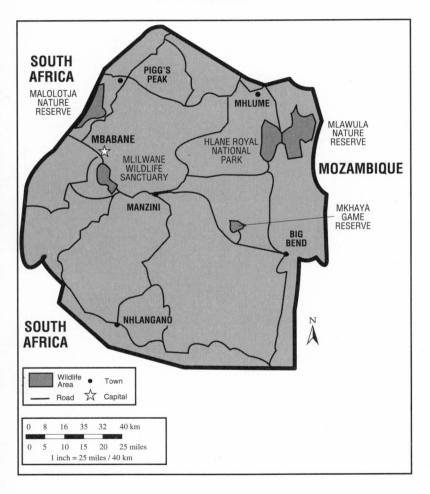

Tanzania

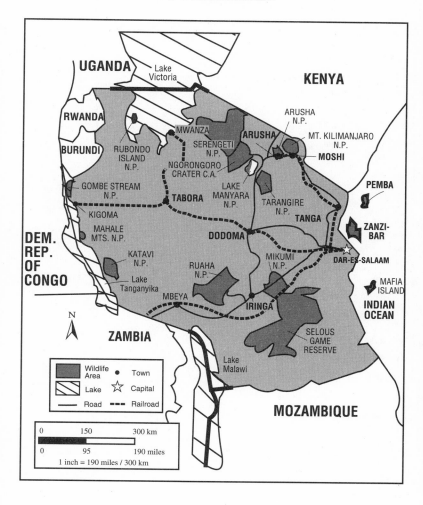

Northern Tanzania

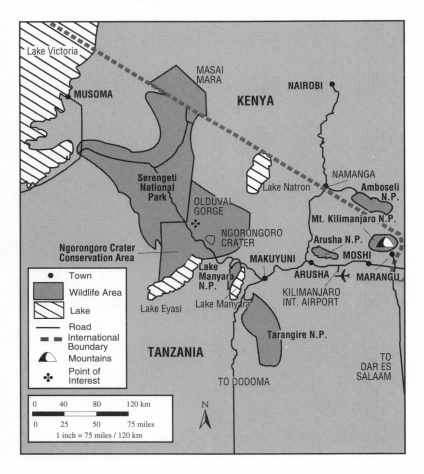

Arusha National Park

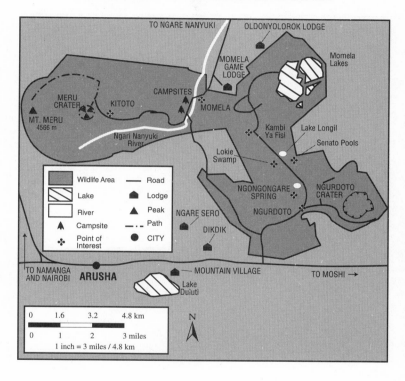

TO NGARE NANYUKI
OLDONYOLOROK LODGE

MOMELA
GAME
LODGE

Momela
Lakes

CAMPSITES

MERU
CRATER
KITOTO
MOMELA

MT. MERU
4566 m

Ngari Nanyuki
River

Kambi
Ya Fisi
Lake Longil

Senato Pools

Lokie
Swamp

NGONGONGARE
SPRING
NGURDOTO
CRATER

NGARE SERO
NGURDOTO

DIKDIK

▨ Wildlife Area	— Road
▨ Lake	🏠 Lodge
☐ River	▲ Peak
⚑ Campsite	–·– Path
✿ Point of Interest	● CITY

TO NAMANGA
AND NAIROBI
ARUSHA
MOUNTAIN VILLAGE
TO MOSHI →

Lake
Duluti

0   1.6   3.2   4.8 km

0   1   2   3 miles

1 inch = 3 miles / 4.8 km

N

Lake Manyara National Park

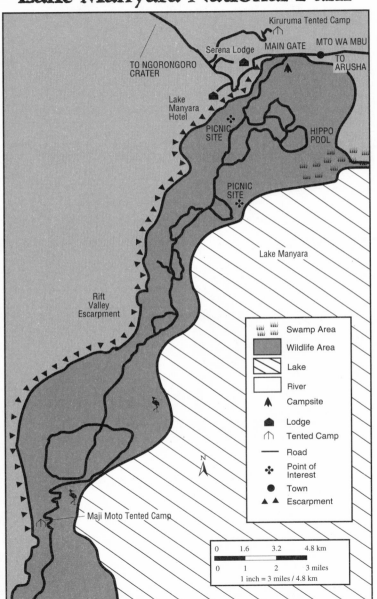

Ngorongoro Crater

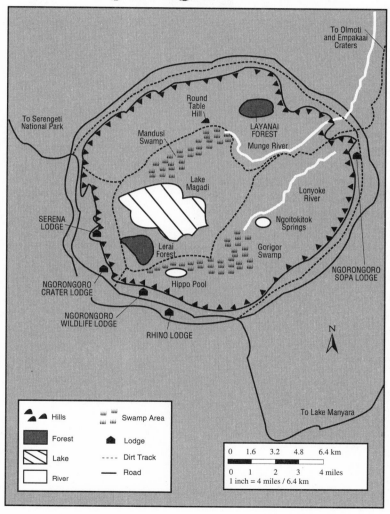

To Olmoti
and Empakaai
Craters

To Serengeti
National Park

Round
Table
Hill

LAYANAI
FOREST

Mandusi
Swamp

Munge River

Lake
Magadi

Lonyoke
River

Ngoitokitok
Springs

SERENA
LODGE

Lerai
Forest

Gorigor
Swamp

NGORONGORO
SOPA LODGE

NGORONGORO
CRATER LODGE

Hippo Pool

NGORONGORO
WILDLIFE LODGE

RHINO LODGE

N

To Lake Manyara

Hills

Swamp Area

Forest

Lodge

Lake

---- **Dirt Track**

River

—— **Road**

| 0 | 1.6 | 3.2 | 4.8 | 6.4 km |

| 0 | 1 | 2 | 3 | 4 miles |

1 inch = 4 miles / 6.4 km

119

Serengeti National Park

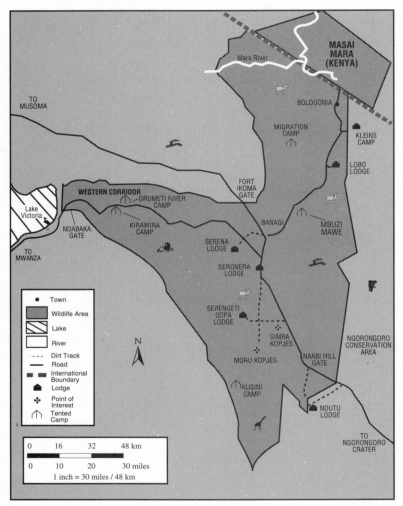

The Great Serengeti Migration

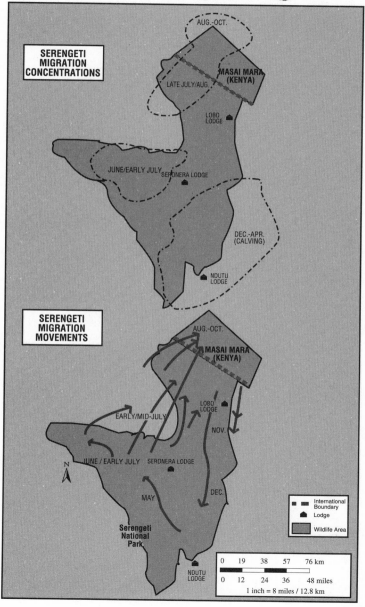

SERENGETI
MIGRATION
CONCENTRATIONS

AUG.-OCT.

MASAI MARA
(KENYA)

LATE JULY/AUG.

LOBO
LODGE

JUNE/EARLY JULY SERONERA LODGE

DEC.-APR.
(CALVING)

NDUTU
LODGE

SERENGETI
MIGRATION
MOVEMENTS

AUG.-OCT.

MASAI MARA
(KENYA)

LOBO
LODGE

EARLY/MID-JULY

NOV.

N

JUNE / EARLY JULY SERONERA LODGE

MAY

DEC.

Serengeti
National
Park

International
Boundary

Lodge

Wildlife Area

0	19	38	57	76 km
0	12	24	36	48 miles

1 inch = 8 miles / 12.8 km

NDUTU
LODGE

Tarangire National Park

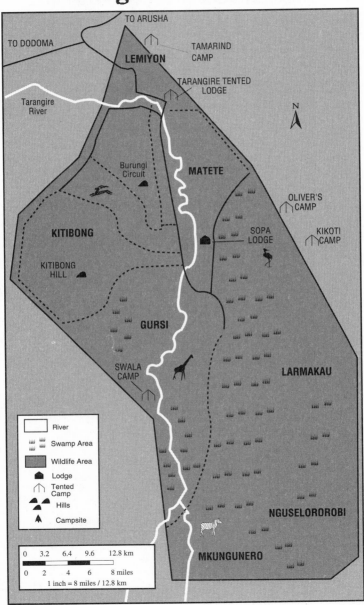

TO ARUSHA

TO DODOMA

LEMIYON

TAMARIND CAMP

TARANGIRE TENTED LODGE

Tarangire River

N

Burungi Circuit

MATETE

OLIVER'S CAMP

KITIBONG

SOPA LODGE

KIKOTI CAMP

KITIBONG HILL

GURSI

SWALA CAMP

LARMAKAU

	River
	Swamp Area
	Wildlife Area
	Lodge
	Tented Camp
	Hills
	Campsite

NGUSELORORORBI

MKUNGUNERO

0	3.2	6.4	9.6	12.8 km
0	2	4	6	8 miles

1 inch = 8 miles / 12.8 km

Routes on Mt. Kilimanjaro

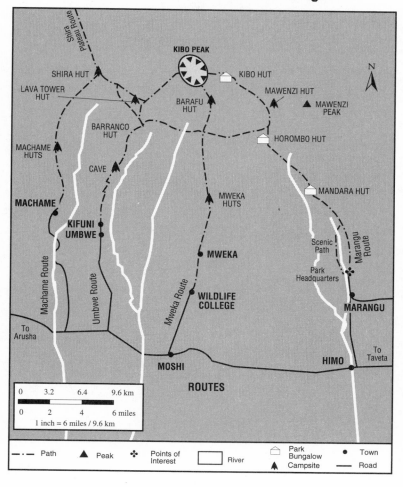

Shira Route
Plateau Route

KIBO PEAK

SHIRA HUT
KIBO HUT

LAVA TOWER HUT
MAWENZI HUT

BARAFU HUT
MAWENZI PEAK

BARRANCO HUT
HOROMBO HUT

MACHAME HUTS

CAVE

MANDARA HUT

MWEKA HUTS

MACHAME

KIFUNI UMBWE

Scenic Path

Marangu Route

MWEKA

Park Headquarters

Machame Route

Umbwe Route

Mweka Route

WILDLIFE COLLEGE

MARANGU

To Arusha

To Taveta

MOSHI

HIMO

ROUTES

0	3.2	6.4	9.6 km
0	2	4	6 miles

1 inch = 6 miles / 9.6 km

–·– Path   ▲ Peak   ✣ Points of Interest   ⬡ River   ⌂ Park Bungalow   ▲ Campsite   ● Town   — Road

N

123

Kibo Peak
Mt. Kilimanjaro

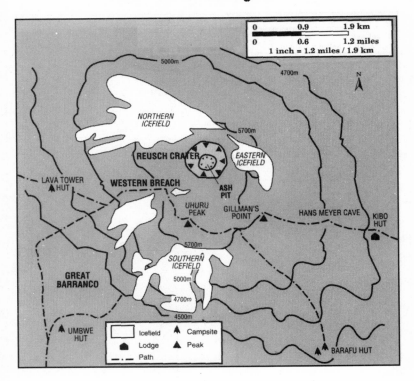

Uganda

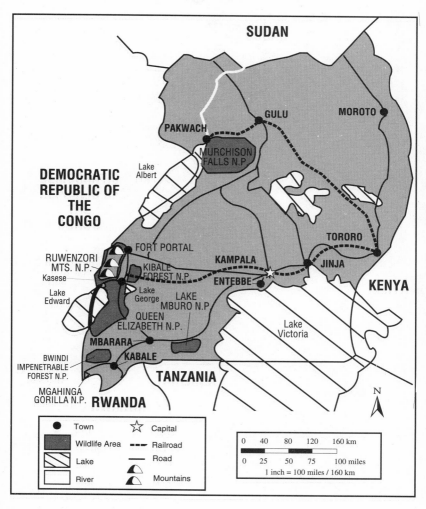

Queen Elizabeth National Park

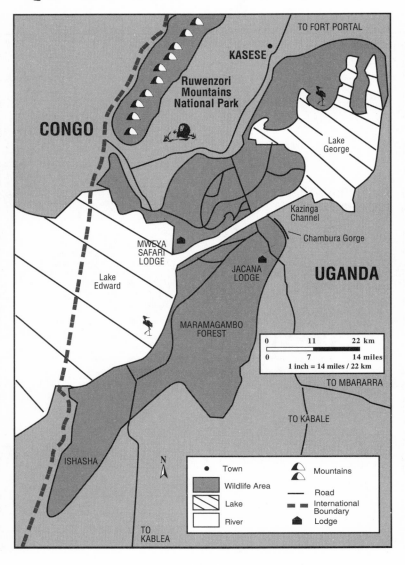

TO FORT PORTAL

KASESE

Ruwenzori
Mountains
National Park

CONGO

Lake
George

Kazinga
Channel

Chambura Gorge

MWEYA
SAFARI
LODGE

JACANA
LODGE

UGANDA

Lake
Edward

MARAMAGAMBO
FOREST

0	11	22 km
0	7	14 miles

1 inch = 14 miles / 22 km

TO MBARARRA

TO KABALE

ISHASHA

N

Town		Mountains
Wildlife Area		Road
Lake		International Boundary
River		Lodge

TO
KABLEA

Ruwenzori Mountains

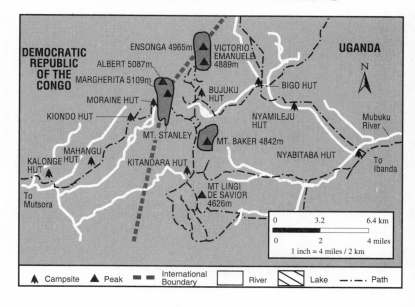

DEMOCRATIC REPUBLIC OF THE CONGO

ENSONGA 4965m

VICTORIO EMANUELE 4889m

UGANDA

N

ALBERT 5087m

MARGHERITA 5109m

BUJUKU HUT

BIGO HUT

MORAINE HUT

NYAMILEJU HUT

Mubuku River

KIONDO HUT

MT. STANLEY

MT. BAKER 4842m

MAHANGU HUT

NYABITABA HUT

KALONGE HUT

KITANDARA HUT

To Ibanda

To Mutsora

MT LINGI DE SAVIOR 4626m

0	3.2	6.4 km
0	2	4 miles

1 inch = 4 miles / 2 km

▲ Campsite ▲ Peak ▪▪ ▪▪ International Boundary ☐ River ◫ Lake —·—· Path

Zambia

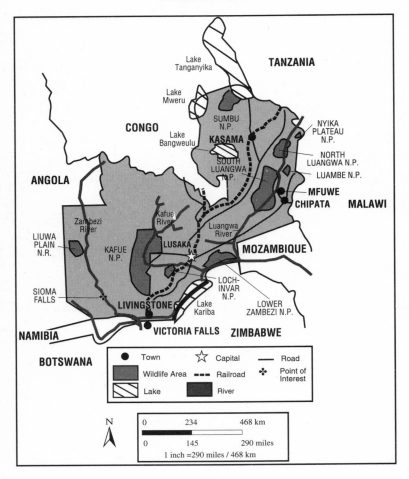

South Luangwa National Park

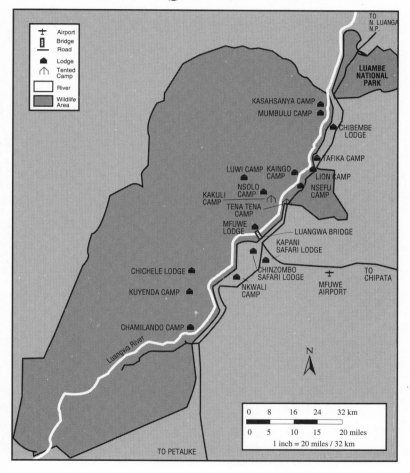

Kafue National Park

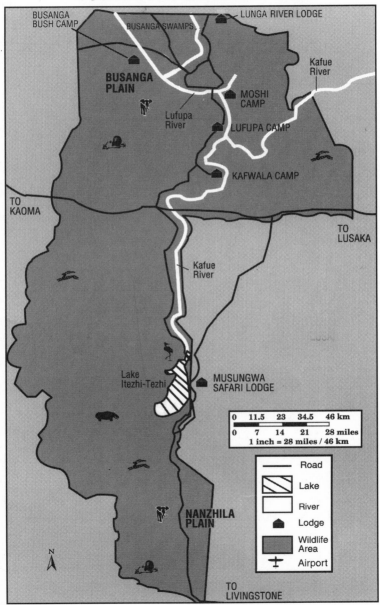

BUSANGA
BUSH CAMP

LUNGA RIVER LODGE

BUSANGA SWAMPS

Kafue
River

BUSANGA
PLAIN

MOSHI
CAMP

Lufupa
River

LUFUPA CAMP

KAFWALA CAMP

TO
KAOMA

TO
LUSAKA

Kafue
River

Lake
Itezhi-Tezhi

MUSUNGWA
SAFARI LODGE

0	11.5	23	34.5	46 km
0	7	14	21	28 miles

1 inch = 28 miles / 46 km

	Road
	Lake
	River
	Lodge
	Wildlife Area
✈	Airport

NANZHILA
PLAIN

N

TO
LIVINGSTONE

Lower Zambezi National Park

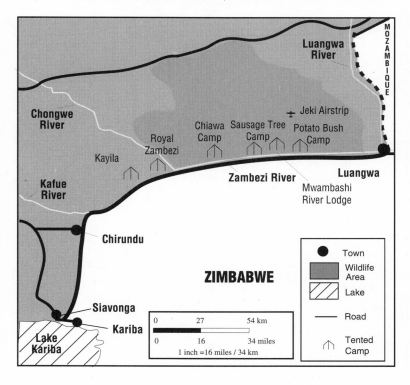

Zimbabwe

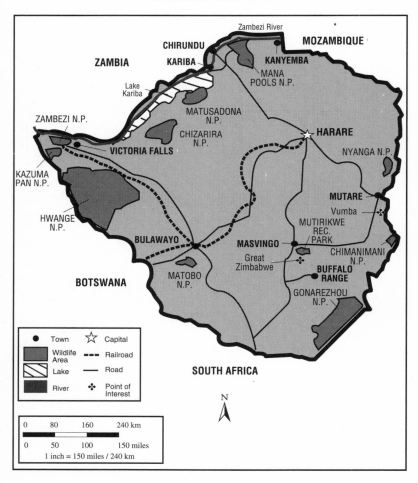

ZAMBIA

CHIRUNDU

KARIBA

Zambezi River

MOZAMBIQUE

KANYEMBA

MANA POOLS N.P.

Lake Kariba

MATUSADONA N.P.

CHIZARIRA N.P.

ZAMBEZI N.P.

VICTORIA FALLS

HARARE

NYANGA N.P.

KAZUMA PAN N.P.

HWANGE N.P.

MUTARE

Vumba

MUTIRIKWE REC. PARK

BULAWAYO

MASVINGO

CHIMANIMANI N.P.

Great Zimbabwe

BUFFALO RANGE

MATOBO N.P.

BOTSWANA

GONAREZHOU N.P.

SOUTH AFRICA

N

● Town	☆ Capital
Wildlife Area	--- Railroad
Lake	— Road
River	❖ Point of Interest

0	80	160	240 km
0	50	100	150 miles

1 inch = 150 miles / 240 km

Northwest Zimbabwe

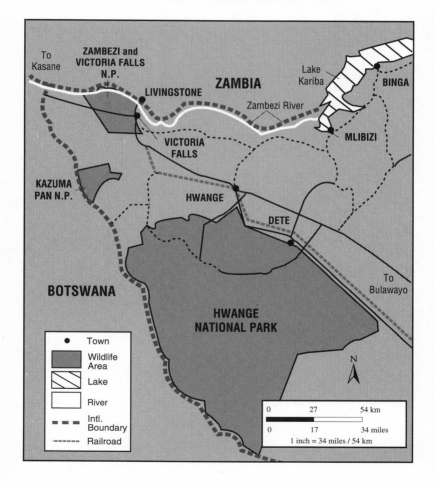

Hwange National Park

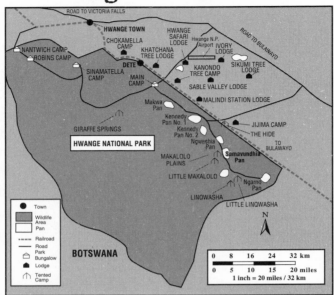

Matusadona National Park

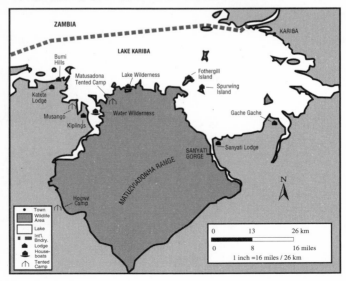

Mana Pools National Park

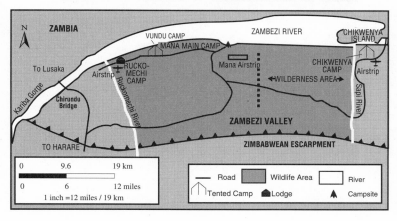

Photographic
Record

Photographic Record

Roll number: _____
Film type/ASA: _____
Date(s) shot: _____
Description: _____
_____
_____
_____

Roll number: _____
Film type/ASA: _____
Date(s) shot: _____
Description: _____
_____
_____
_____

Roll number: _____
Film type/ASA: _____
Date(s) shot: _____
Description: _____
_____
_____
_____

Roll number: _____
Film type/ASA: _____
Date(s) shot: _____
Description: _____
_____
_____
_____

Roll number: _____
Film type/ASA: _____
Date(s) shot: _____
Description: _____
_____
_____
_____

Photographic Record

Roll number: _____
Film type/ASA: _____
Date(s) shot: _____
Description: _____
_____
_____
_____

Roll number: _____
Film type/ASA: _____
Date(s) shot: _____
Description: _____
_____
_____
_____

Roll number: _____
Film type/ASA: _____
Date(s) shot: _____
Description: _____
_____
_____
_____

Roll number: _____
Film type/ASA: _____
Date(s) shot: _____
Description: _____
_____
_____
_____

Roll number: _____
Film type/ASA: _____
Date(s) shot: _____
Description: _____
_____
_____
_____

Photographic Record

Roll number: _____
Film type/ASA: _____
Date(s) shot: _____
Description: _____
_____
_____
_____

Roll number: _____
Film type/ASA: _____
Date(s) shot: _____
Description: _____
_____
_____
_____

Roll number: _____
Film type/ASA: _____
Date(s) shot: _____
Description: _____
_____
_____
_____

Roll number: _____
Film type/ASA: _____
Date(s) shot: _____
Description: _____
_____
_____
_____

Roll number: _____
Film type/ASA: _____
Date(s) shot: _____
Description: _____
_____
_____
_____

Photographic Record

Roll number: _____
Film type/ASA: _____
Date(s) shot: _____
Description: _____
_____
_____

Roll number: _____
Film type/ASA: _____
Date(s) shot: _____
Description: _____
_____
_____

Roll number: _____
Film type/ASA: _____
Date(s) shot: _____
Description: _____
_____
_____

Roll number: _____
Film type/ASA: _____
Date(s) shot: _____
Description: _____
_____
_____

Roll number: _____
Film type/ASA: _____
Date(s) shot: _____
Description: _____
_____
_____

Photographic Record

Roll number: _____
Film type/ASA: _____
Date(s) shot: _____
Description: _____
_____
_____

Roll number: _____
Film type/ASA: _____
Date(s) shot: _____
Description: _____
_____
_____

Roll number: _____
Film type/ASA: _____
Date(s) shot: _____
Description: _____
_____
_____

Roll number: _____
Film type/ASA: _____
Date(s) shot: _____
Description: _____
_____
_____

Roll number: _____
Film type/ASA: _____
Date(s) shot: _____
Description: _____
_____
_____

Photographic Record

Roll number: _____
Film type/ASA: _____
Date(s) shot: _____
Description: _____
_____
_____
_____

Roll number: _____
Film type/ASA: _____
Date(s) shot: _____
Description: _____
_____
_____

Roll number: _____
Film type/ASA: _____
Date(s) shot: _____
Description: _____
_____
_____

Roll number: _____
Film type/ASA: _____
Date(s) shot: _____
Description: _____
_____
_____

Roll number: _____
Film type/ASA: _____
Date(s) shot: _____
Description: _____
_____
_____

Photographic Record

Roll number: _____
Film type/ASA: _____
Date(s) shot: _____
Description: _____
_____
_____
_____

Roll number: _____
Film type/ASA: _____
Date(s) shot: _____
Description: _____
_____
_____
_____

Roll number: _____
Film type/ASA: _____
Date(s) shot: _____
Description: _____
_____
_____
_____

Roll number: _____
Film type/ASA: _____
Date(s) shot: _____
Description: _____
_____
_____
_____

Roll number: _____
Film type/ASA: _____
Date(s) shot: _____
Description: _____
_____
_____
_____

African
SAFARI JOURNAL

Photographic Record

Roll number: _____
Film type/ASA: _____
Date(s) shot: _____
Description: _____
_____
_____
_____

Roll number: _____
Film type/ASA: _____
Date(s) shot: _____
Description: _____
_____
_____
_____

Roll number: _____
Film type/ASA: _____
Date(s) shot: _____
Description: _____
_____
_____
_____

Roll number: _____
Film type/ASA: _____
Date(s) shot: _____
Description: _____
_____
_____
_____

Roll number: _____
Film type/ASA: _____
Date(s) shot: _____
Description: _____
_____
_____
_____

Photographic Record

Roll number: _____
Film type/ASA: _____
Date(s) shot: _____
Description: _____
_____
_____
_____

Roll number: _____
Film type/ASA: _____
Date(s) shot: _____
Description: _____
_____
_____
_____

Roll number: _____
Film type/ASA: _____
Date(s) shot: _____
Description: _____
_____
_____
_____

Roll number: _____
Film type/ASA: _____
Date(s) shot: _____
Description: _____
_____
_____
_____

Roll number: _____
Film type/ASA: _____
Date(s) shot: _____
Description: _____
_____
_____
_____

Photographic Record

Roll number: _____
Film type/ASA: _____
Date(s) shot: _____
Description: _____
_____
_____
_____

Roll number: _____
Film type/ASA: _____
Date(s) shot: _____
Description: _____
_____
_____
_____

Roll number: _____
Film type/ASA: _____
Date(s) shot: _____
Description: _____
_____
_____
_____

Roll number: _____
Film type/ASA: _____
Date(s) shot: _____
Description: _____
_____
_____
_____

Roll number: _____
Film type/ASA: _____
Date(s) shot: _____
Description: _____
_____
_____
_____

Photographic Record

Roll number: _____
Film type/ASA: _____
Date(s) shot: _____
Description: _____
_____
_____

Roll number: _____
Film type/ASA: _____
Date(s) shot: _____
Description: _____
_____
_____

Roll number: _____
Film type/ASA: _____
Date(s) shot: _____
Description: _____
_____
_____

Roll number: _____
Film type/ASA: _____
Date(s) shot: _____
Description: _____
_____
_____

Roll number: _____
Film type/ASA: _____
Date(s) shot: _____
Description: _____
_____
_____

Journal
Entries

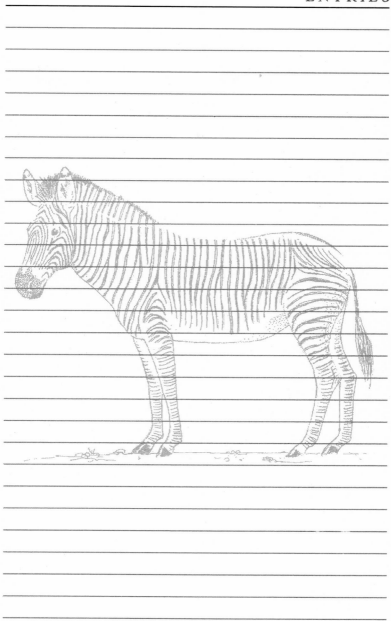

Languages

Swahili Words and Phrases
(KENYA, TANZANIA AND UGANDA)

GENERAL EXPRESSIONS

English	Swahili	Phonetics
hello	jambo	jä-mbô
How are you?	Habari?	hä-bä-ree
fine, good	nzuri	nzoo-ree
good-bye	kwaheri	kwä-hay-ree
mister	bwana	bwä-nä
madam	bibi	bee-bee
yes/no	ndio/hapana	ndee-ô/hä-pä-nä
please	tafadhali	itä-fä-dhä-lee
thank you	asante	ä-sä-ntay
very much	sana	sä-nä
today	leo	lay-ô
tomorrow	kesho	kay-shô
yesterday	jana	jä-nä
toilet	choo	chô-ô
left	kushoto	koo-shô-tô
right	kulia	koo-lee-ä
I want	nataka	nä-tä-kä
I would like	ningependa	nee-ngay-pee-ndä
How much?	Pesa ngapi?	pay-sä ngä-pee
How many?	Ngapi?	ngä-pee
Where is?	Iko wapi?	ee-kô wä-pee
When?	Lini?	lee-nee
to eat	kula	koo-lä
food	chakula	chä-koo-lä
water	maji	mä-jee
coffee	kahawa	kä-hä-wä
tea	chai	chä-ee
milk	maziwa	mä-zee-wä
beer	pombe	pô-mbay
bread	mkate	'm-kä-tay
butter	siagi	see-ä-gee
sugar	sukari	soo-kä-ree
salt	chumvi	choo-'m-vee
hot/fire	moto	mô-tô
cold	baridi	bä-ree-dee
ice	barafu	bä-rä-foo

NUMBERS

English	Swahili	Phonetics
one	moja	mô-jä
two	mbili	mbee-lee
three	tatu	tä-too
four	nne	'n-nay
five	tano	tä-nô
six	sita	see-tä
seven	saba	sä-bä
eight	nane	nä-nay
nine	tisa	tee-sä
ten	kumi	koo-mee
eleven	kumi na moja	koo-mee nä mô-jä
twenty	ishirini	eé-shee-ree-nee
thirty	thelathini	thay-lä-thee-nee
forty	arobaini	ä-rô-bä-ee-nee
fifty	hamsini	hä-m'-see-nee
sixty	sitini	see'-tee-nee
seventy	sabini	sä'-bee-nee
eighty	themanini	thay-mä-nee-nee
ninety	tisini	tee'-see-nee
hundred	mia	mee-ä
thousand	elf	ay-l'-foo

MAMMAL NAMES

English	Swahili	Phonetics
aardvark	muhanga	moo-hä-ngä
aardwolf	fisi ndogo	fee-see ndô-gô
antelope, roan	korongo	kô-rô-ngô
antelope, sable	palahala	pä-lä-hä-lä
baboon	nyani	nyä-nee
buffalo	nyati	nyä-tee
bushbaby	komba	kô-mbä
bushbuck	pongo	pô-ngô
bushpig	nguruwe	ngoo-roo-way
caracal	siba mangu	see-bä mä-ngoo
cheetah	duma	doo-mä
chimpanzee	sokwe mtu	sô-kway 'm-too
civet	fungo	foo-ngô
dikdik	dikidiki	dee-kee-dee-kee
duiker	naya	n-syä
eland	pofu	pô-foo
elephant	tembo	tay-mbô
fox, bat-eared	mbweha masikio	mbway-hä mä-see-ke
gazelle, Grant's	swala granti	swä-lä 'grä-ntee
gazelle, Thomson's	swala tomi	swä-lä tô-mee
genet	kanu	kä-noo
giraffe	nguruwe, twiga	ngoo-roo-way, twee-gä
gorilla	makaku	mä-kä-koo
hare	sungura	soo-ngoo-rä
hartebeest	kongoni	kô-ngô-nee
hedgehog	kalunguyeye	kä-loo-ngoo-yay-yay

MAMMAL NAMES

English	Swahili	Phonetics
hippopotamus	kiboko	kee-bô-kô
hog, giant forest	nguruwe mwitu dume	ngoo-roo-we mwe-too doo-may
honey badger	nyegere	nyay-gay-ray
hyena	fisi	fee-see
hyrax	pimbi	pee-mbee
impala	swalapala	swä-lä-pä-lä
jackal	mbweha	mbway-hä
klipspringer	mbuzimawe	mboo-zee-mä-wee
kudu	tandala mdogo	tä-ndä-lä 'm-dô-gô
leopard	chi	choo-ee
lion	simba	see-mbä
mongoose	nguchiro	ngoo-chee-rô
monkey, colobus	mbega	mbay-gä
monkey, vervet	tumbili ngedere	too-mbee-lee ngay-day-ray
oribi	taya	tä-yä
oryx	choroa	chô-rô-ä
otter	fisi maji	fee-see mä-jee
pangolin	kakakuona	kä-kä-koo-ô-nä
porcupine	nunguri	noo-ngoo-ray
reedbuck	tohe	tô-hay
rhino	kifaru	kee-fä-roo
serval	mondo	mô-ndô
sitatunga	nzohe	nzô-hay
squirrel	kidiri	kee-dee-ree
steenbok	dondoro	dô-ndô-rô
topi	nyamera	nyä-may-rä
tsessebe	nyamera	nyä-may-rä
warthog	ngiri	ngee-ree
waterbuck	kuro	koo-rô
wild dog	mbwa mwitu	'mbwä mwee-too
wildebeest	nyumbu	nyoo-mboo
zebra	pundamilia	poo-nday-'mee-lee-ä
zorilla	kicheche	kee-chay-chay

Shona Words and Phrases
(ZIMBABWE)

GENERAL EXPRESSIONS

English	Shona	Phonetics
good morning	mangwanani	mä-gwä-nä'-nee
good day	masikati	mä-see-kä'-tee
good night	manheru	män-ay'-roo
How are you?	Makadini?	mä-kä-dee'-nee
very well	ndiripo zvangu	n-dee-ree'-po zwän'-goo
good-bye (go well)	chiendal zvenyu	chee-aan'-däee zwaan'-yoo
mister	baba	bä'-bä
madam	amai	ä-mä'-yee
yes/no	hongu/kwete	oon'-goo/kwâ-tâ
please	ndapota	n-dä-po'-tä
thank you	mazviita	mä-zwee'-tä
very much	kwazvo	kwä'-zo
today	nhasi	nää'-zee
tomorrow	mangwana	män-gwä-nä
yesterday	nezuro	nay-zoo-rö
toilet	chimbuzi	cheem-boo-zee
left	ruboshwa	roo-bô'-shwâ
right	rudyi	roo'-dee
I want	ndinoda	ndee-no'-dä
How much?	Zvakawanda sei?	zwä-kä-wän'-dä
How many?	Zvingani?	zween-gä-nee
Where is?	Ndekupi?	nday-koo'-pee
When?	Rini?	ree'-nee
to eat	kudya	koo'-deeä
food	chidyo	chee'-deeo
water	mvura	m-voo'-rä
coffee	kofi	ko'-fee
tea	tii	tee
milk	mukaka	moo-kä'-kä
beer	doro	do'-ro
bread	chingwa	cheen'-gwä
butter	bhata	bää'-tä
sugar	shuga, tsvigiri	shoo'-gä, tswee-gee'-ree
salt	munyu	moon'-yoo
hot/fire	inopisa/moto	e-no-pee'-sä/mo'-to
cold	inotonhora	e-no-ton-o-rä
ice	chando, aizi	chän'-do, äee'-zee

NUMBERS

English	Shona	Phonetics
one	potsi	po'-tsee
two	piri	pee'-ree
three	tatu	tä'-too
four	ini	e'-nee
five	shanu	shä'-noo
six	tanhatu	tän-ä-too
seven	nomwe	no'-mway
eight	tsere	tsay'-ray
nine	pfumbanmwe	foom-bä'-mway
ten	gumi	goo'-mee
eleven	gumi nerimwechere	goo'-mee nay-ray-mway'-ayayray
twenty	makumi maviri	mä-koo-mee mä-vee'-ree
thirty	makumi matatu	mä-koo-mee mä-tä'-too
forty	makumi mana	mä-koo-mee mä'-nä
fifty	makumi mashanu	mä-koo-mee mä-shä'-noo
sixty	makumi matanhatu	mä-koo-mee mä-tän'-ä-too
seventy	makumi manomwe	mä-koo-mee mä-no'-mway
eighty	makumi masere	mä-koo-mee mä-say'-ray
ninety	makumi mapfumbamwe	mä-koo-mee mä-foom-bä'-mway
hundred	zana	zä'-nä
thousand	chiuru	chee-oo'-roo

MAMMAL NAMES

English	Shona	Phonetics
aardvark	bikita, chikokoma	bee-kee'-tä, chee-ko-ko'-mä
aardwolf	mwena	mwi-nä
antelope, roan	chengu, ndunguza	chayn'-goo, n-doon-goo'-zä
antelope, sable	mharapara	m-ä'-rä-pä-rä
baboon	bveni/gudo	vay'-nee/goo'-doe
buffalo	nyati	n-yä-tee
bushbaby	chinhavira	cheen-ä-vee'-rä
bushbuck	dzoma	zoo'-mä
bushpig	humba	hoom'-bä
caracal	hwana, twana	hwä-nä, twä-nä
cheetah	didingwe	dee-deen'-gway
civet	bvungo, jachacha	voon'-go, zhä-chä'-chä
duiker	mhembwo	maym'-bway
eland	mhofu	m-o'-foo
elephant	nzou	nzo'-oo
genet	tsimba, simba	tseem'-bä, seem'-bä
giraffe	furiramudenga	foo-ree'-rä-moo-dayn'-gä
hare	tsuro	tsoo'-ro
hartebeest	hwiranondo	whee-rä-nôn'-dô
hedgehog	shoni, tyoni	sho'-nee, too'-nee
hippopotamus	mvuu	m-voo'
honey badger	sere, tsere	say'-ray, tsay'-ray
hyena	bere, magondo	bay'-ray, mä-gôn'-do

MAMMAL NAMES

English	Shona	Phonetics
hyrax	mbira	m-be'-rä
impala	mhara	m-ä-rä
jackal	hungubwe	hoon-goo'-bwa
klipspringer	ngururu	n-goo-roo'-roo
kudu	nhoro	n-o'-ro
leopard	mbada	m-bä'-dä
lion	shumba	shoom'-bä
mongoose	hovo	ho'-vo
monkey, vervet	shoko, tsoko	sho'-ko, tso'-ko
nyala	nyara	n-yä'-rä
oribi	sinza, tsinza	seen'-zä, tseen'-zä
otter	binza, chipu, mbiti	been'-zä, chee'-poo, m-be'-tee
pangolin	haka	hä'-kä
porcupine	nungu	noon'-goo
reedbuck	bimha	beem'-hä
rhino	chipembere	chee-paym-bay-ray
serval	nzudzi, nzunza	n-zoo'-zhee, n-zoon'-zä
squirrel	tsindi	tseen'-dee
steenbok	mhene	m-â-nâ
tsessebe	nondo	non'-do
warthog	njiri	n-zhee'-ree
waterbuck	dhumukwa	doo-moo'-kwä
wild dog	mhumbi	moom'-bee
wildebeest	mvumba, ngongoni	m-voom-bä,n-gon-go'-nee
zebra	mbizi	m-be-ze
zorilla	chidembo	chee-daym'-bo

Tswana Words and Phrases
(BOTSWANA)

GENERAL EXPRESSIONS

English	Tswana	Phonetics
good morning	dumêla	doo-may'-lä
good day	dumêla	doo-may'-lä
good.night	rôbala sentlê	rô-bä'-lä sin'-kla
How are you?	O tsogilê jang?	o tso-khee-lay zhäng
fine, thank you	ke tsogilê sentlê	ki tso-khee-lay sin'-klâ
good-bye (go well)	tsamaya sentlê	tsä-mä-yä sin'-kla
mister	rrê	r-ra'
madam	mmê	m-mô'
yes/no	êê/nnyaa	a'-a/n-nyä'
please	tswêê-tswêê	tswâ-tswâ
thank you	kea lêboga	ki'-ä lay-bo'-khä
very much	thata	tä'-tä
today	gompiêno	khom-pee-a'-no
tomorrow	kamosô	kä-mo'-sô
yesterday	maabane	mä-ä-bä'-ni
toilet	ntlwana ya boithomêlô	n-klwä'-nä yä bo-ee-toe-mô-lo
left	ntlha ya molêma	n-klhä yä mo-lô'-mä
right	ntlha ya go ja	n-klhä yä kho zhä
I want	ke batla	ki bä-klä
How much?	Bokae?	bo-kä'-i
How many?	Dikae?	dee-kä'-i
Which way is?	Tsela e kae?	tsela-a-kä'-i
When?	Leng?	li'-ng
to eat	go ja	kho zhä
food	dijô	dee'-zhô
water	mêtsi	may-tsee'
coffee	kôfi	ko'-fee
tea	tee	ti'-i
milk	maswi/mashi	mä-shwee/mä'-shee
beer	bojalwa	bo-zhä'-lwä
bread	borôthô	bo-rô'-tô
butter	bôtôrô	bô-tô'-rô
sugar	sukiri	soo-kee'-ree
salt	letswai	li-tswä'-ee
fire (hot)	aa fisa/molelô	ä'-ä fee-sä/mo-li'-lô
cold	a tsididi	ä tsee-dee'-dee
ice	segagane	see-khä-khä'-ni

NUMBERS

English	Tswana	Phonetics
one	nngwe	n-ngwâ'
two	pedi	pay'-dee
three	tharo	tä'-ro
four	nne	n-nâ'
five	tlhano	klhä'-no
six	thataro	tä-tä'-ro
seven	supa	soo'-pä
eight	rôbêdi	ro-bay'-dee
nine	rôbongwe	ro-bo'-ngwâ
ten	lesomê	li-so'-mâ
eleven	lesomê le motsô	li-so'-mâ li mo-tsô
twenty	masomê mabêdi	mä-so'-mâ ä mä-bay'-de
thirty	masomê mararo	mä-so'-mâ ä mä-rä'-ro
forty	masomê manê	mä-so'-mâ ä mä'-nâ
fifty	masomê amatlhano	mä-so'-mâ ä mä-klhä'-no
sixty	masomê amarataro	mä-so'-mâ ä mä-rä-tä'-ro
seventy	masomê aa supa	mä-so'-mâ ä soo-pä
eighty	maomê aa rôbêdi	mä-so'-mâ ä ro-bay'-dee
ninety	masomê aa rôbongwe	mä-so'-mâ ä ro-bo-ngwe
hundred	lekgolo	li-kho'-lo
thousand	sekete	si-ki'-ti

MAMMAL NAMES

English	Tswana	Phonetics
aardvark	thakadu	tä-kä-doo
aardwolf	thukhwi	too-khwee
antelope, roan	kwalara êtsnêtiha	kw-lä-tä a tsâ'-klhä
antelope, sable	kwalata êntsho	kwä-lä'-tä a n-cho'
baboon	tshwêne	chway'-ni
buffalo	nare	nä'-ri
bushbaby	mogwele	mo-khwi'-li
bushbuck	serôlô-bolhoko	si-rô'-lô-bo-klo-ko
bushpig	kolobê	ko-lo'-bâ
caracal	thwane	twä'-ni
cheetah	letlôtse	li-ngä'-oo li-klô-tsâ
civet	tshipalore	tse-pä-lo-ri
duiker	photi	poo'-tee
eland	phôhu	po'-foo/po'-hoo
elephant	tlôu	klo'-oo
fox, bat-eared	(mo)tlhose	(mo) klho'-si
genet	tshipa	tse-pä
giraffe	thutlwa	too'-klwä
hare	mmutla	m-moo'-klä
hartebeest	kgama	khä'-mä
hedgehog	(se)tlhông	(si) klho'-ng
hippopotamus	kubu	koo'-boo
honey badger	magôgwê/matshwane	mä-khô-khwâ/mä-chwä'-ni

MAMMAL NAMES

English	Tswana	Phonetics
hyena, spotted	phiri	pe'-re
hyrax	pela	pi'-lä
impala	phala	pä'-lä
jackal	phokojwê	po-ko-zhwâ
klipspringer	mokabayane, kololo	mo-kä-bä-yä'-ni, ko-lo'-lo
kudu	thôlô	tô'-lô
lechwe	letswee	li-tswi'-i
leopard	nkwê	n-kwâ
lion	tau	tä'-oo
mongoose, slender	kgano	khä'-no
monkey, vervet	kgabo	khä'-bo
oribi	phuduhudu kgamane	poo-doo-hoo-doo khä-mä-ni
oryx	kukama	koo-kä'-mä
otter	kônyana yanoka	kôn-yä-nä yä-no-kä
pangolin	kgaga	khä'-khä
porcupine	noko	no'-ko
reedbuck	sebogata, motsweema	si-boo'-gä-tä, mo-tsway-ay-mä
rhino	tshukudu	choo-koo'-doo
serval	tadi	tä'-de
sitatunga	sitatunga/nankông	si-tä-toon'-gä/nân-ko'-ng
springbok	tshêphê	tsâ'-pâ
squirrel, tree	setlhora	si-klho'-rä
steenbok	phuduhudu	poo-doo-hoo'-doo
tsessebe	tshêsêbê	tsâ-sâ-bâ
warthog	kolobê yanaga	ko-lo-bâ yä nä'-khä
waterbuck	motumoga	mo-too-mo'-khä
wild dog	letlhalerwa	li-klhä-li-rwä
wildebeest, blue	kgôkông	kho-ko'-ng
zebra	pitse/yanaga	pe'-tsi
zorilla	nakêdi	nä-kay-dee

Zulu Words and Phrases
(SOUTH AFRICA)

GENERAL EXPRESSIONS

English	Zulu	Phonetics
good morning	sawubona	sä-woo'-bo-nä
good day	sawubona	sä-woo'-bo-nä
good night	lala kahle	lä-lä kä'-klhay
How are you?	Kunjani?	koon-zhä'-nee
very well	kuhle	koo'-klhay
good-bye (go well)	hamba kahle	häm'-bä kä-klhay
mister	mnumzane	m-noom-zä-ni
madam	nkosazane	n-ko-s-ä-zä'-ni
yes/no	yebo/qua	yay'-bo/qwa
please	ngiyacela	n-gee-yä-câ'-lä
thank you	ngiyabonga	n-gee-yä-bon-gä
very much	kakhulu	kä-koo'-loo
today	namuhla	nä-moo'-klhä
tomorrow	kusasa	koo'-sä-sä
yesterday	izolo	e-zo'-lo
toilet	indlwana	een-dlwä'-nä
	yangaphandle	yän-gä-pän'-dlee
left	esokunxele	i-so-koo-nxay'-lay
right	esokudia	i-so-koo'-dlä
I want	ngifuna	n-gee-foo'-nä
How much?	Kangakanani?	kän-gä-kä-nä'-nee
How many?	Zingakanani?	zeen-gä-kä-nä'-nee
Where is?	Zikuphi?	zee-koo'-pee
When?	Nini?	nee'-nee
to eat	ukudla	oo-koo'-dlä
food	ukudla	oo-koo'-dlä
water	amanzi	ä-män'-zee
coffee	ikhofi	e-ko'-fee
tea	itiye	e-tee'-yay
milk	ubisi	oo-be'-see
beer	utshwala, ubhiya	oo-chwä'-lä, oo-be'-yä
bread	isinkwa	e-seen'-kwä
butter	ibhotela	e-bo-tay'-lä
sugar	ushukela	oo-shoo'-kay-lä
salt	itswayi, usawoti	e-tswä'-e, oo-sä-oo-tee
hot/fire	ayashisa/umlilo	ä-yä-she'-sä/oom-lee'-lo
cold	ayabanda	ä-yä-bän'-dä
ice	iqhwa	e'-qhwä

NUMBERS

English	Zulu	Phonetics
one	kunye	koon'-yay
two	kubili	koo-be'-lee
three	kutathu	koo-tä'-too
four	kune	koo'-nay
five	kuhlanu	koo-klä'-noo
six	isithupha	e-see-too'-pä
seven	isikhombisa	e-see-kom-be'-sä
eight	isithobambili	e-see-to'-bäm-be-lee
nine	isithobanye	e-see-to'-bän-yay
ten	ishumi	e-shoo'-me
eleven	ishumi nanye	e-shoo'-me nän-yay
twenty	amashumi amabili	ä-mä-shoo'-me ä mä-be'-lee
thirty	amashumi amathathu	ä-mä-shoo'-me ä mä-tä'-too
forty	amashumi amane	ä-mä-shoo'-me ä mä'-nay
fifty	amashumi amahlanu	ä-mä-shoo'-me ä mä-klhä'-noo
sixty	amashumi ayisithupha	ä-mä-shoo'-me ä ye-see-too'-pä
seventy	amashumi ayisikhombisa	ä-mä-shoo'-me ä ye-see-kom-be-sä
eighty	amashumi ayisithobambili	ä-mä-shoo'-me ä ye-see-to-bäm-be'-lee
ninety	amashumi ayisithoba	ä-mä-shoo'-me ä ye-see-to'-bä
hundred	ikhulu	e-koo'-loo
thousand	inkulungwane	een-koo-loon-gwä'-ni

MAMMAL NAMES

English	Zulu	Phonetics
aardvark	isambane	e-säm-bä'-ni
aardwolf	isingci	e-see'-ngcee
antelope, sable	impalampala	eem-pä-läm-pä
baboon	imfene	eem-fay'-nay
buffalo	inyathi	een-yä'-tee
bushbaby	insinkwe	e-seen'-kway
bushbuck	imbabala	eem-bä-bä'-lä
bushpig	ingulube	een-goo-loo'-bay
caracal	indabushe	e-dä-boo-she
cheetah	ingulule	een-goo-loo'-lay
civet	impica	eem-pee'-cä
duiker	impunzi	eem-poon'-zee
eland	impofu	eem-po'-foo
elephant	indlovu	een-dlo'-voo
genet	insimba	en-seem'-bä
giraffe	indiulamithi	een-dloo-lä-me'-tee
hare	unogwaja, umvundla	oo-no-gwä'-zä, oom-voon'-dlä

MAMMAL NAMES

English	Zulu	Phonetics
hartebeest	indluzele, inkolongwane	een-dloo-zay'-lay, eenko-loon-gwä'-ni
hedgehog	inhloni	een-klo'-nee
hippopotamus	imvuvu	eem-voo'-boo
honey badger	insele	een-say'-lay
hyena	impisi	eem-pee'-see
hyrax	imbila	eem-be'-lä
impala	impala	eem-pä'-lä
jackal	impungutshe	eem-poon-goo'-tsee
klipspringer	igogo	e-go'-go
kudu	umgankla	oom-gän'-klä
leopard	ingwa	een'-gwä
lion	ingonyama, ibhubese	een-gon-yä'-mä, e-boo-bay'-see
mongoose	uchakide	oo-chä-kee'-day
monkey, vervet	inkawu	een-kä-woo
nyala	inyala	een-yä'-lä
oribi	iwula	e-woo'-lä
otter	umthini	oom-tee'-nee
pangolin	isambane	e-säm-bä'-ni
porcupine	inungu, ingungumbane	e-noon'-goo, een-goon-goom'-bä-ni
reedbuck	inhlangu	een-klhän'-goo
rhino	umkhombe, ubhejane	oom-koom'-bâ, oo-b-zhä'-ni
serval	indlozi	een-dlo'-zee
springbok	insephe	een-say'-pay
squirrel	intshindane	een-tseen-dä'-ni
steenbok	inqhina	e-qhee'-nä
warthog	indlovudawana, intibane	een-dloo-voo-dä-wä-nä, een-tee-bä'-ni
waterbuck	iphiva	e-pee-vä
wild dog	inkentshane	een-kane-tsä'-ni
wildebeest	inkonkoni	een-kone-ko'-nee
zebra	idube	e-doo'-bay
zorilla	iqaqa	e-qä'-aä

French Words and Phrases
(CENTRAL AFRICA)

GENERAL EXPRESSIONS

English	French	Phonetics
good morning	bon jour	bonjor
good day	bon jour	bonjor
good night	bonne nuit	bon nuee
How are you?	Comment allez-vous?	koman-tallay-voo
very well	très bien	tray-beeuh
good-bye (go well)	au revoir	o-revwour
mister	monsieur	muh seeuh
madam	madame	madam
yes/no	oui/non	wee/no
please	s'il vous plait	seal-voo-play
thank you	merci	mear see
very much	beaucoup	bo-koo
today	aujourd'hui	o jord wee
tomorrow	demain	duhma
yesterday	hier	ee year
toilet	toilette	twalet
left	gauche	gosh
right	droite	drwat
I want	je dèsire	juh dezeer
How much?	Combien?	komb ya
How many?	Combien?	komb ya
Where is?	Ou est?	oo-ay
When?	Quand?	kon
to eat	manger	mon-jay
food	nourriture	nureetur
water	eau	o
coffee	cafè	kafe
tea	thè	te
milk	lait	lay
beer	bière	be-year
bread	pain	pun
butter	beurre	burr
sugar	sucre	sukr
salt	sel	cell
pepper	poivre	pwavr
hot/fire	chaud/feu	show/fuh
cold	froid	frwa
ice	glace	glass

NUMBERS

English	French	Phonetics
one	un	uh
two	deux	duh
three	trois	trwa
four	quatre	katr
five	cinq	sank
six	six	sees
seven	sept	set
eight	huit	wheat
nine	neuf	nuhf
ten	dix	dees
eleven	onze	ownz
twenty	vingt	vuh
thirty	trente	trwant
forty	quarante	karant
fifty	cinquante	sank-ant
sixty	soixante	swa-sant
seventy	soixante-dix	swa-sant dees
eighty	quatre-vingt(s)	katr-vuh
ninety	quatre-vingt(s)-dix	katr-vuh dees
hundred	cent	san
thousand	mille	meal

MAMMAL NAMES

English	French	Phonetics
aardvark	fourmillier	foor mee lye
aardwolf	protèle	protel
antelope, roan	hippotrague rouanne	eepotrahguh-rwan
antelope, sable	hippotrague noir	eepotrahguh-nwar
baboon	babouin	bah bwa
bongo	bongo	bongo
buffalo, Cape	buffle d'Afrique	bufl-dafreek
bushbaby, greater	galago à guelle epaisse	galago-ah-kuh-aypass
bushbuck	antilope harnaché	onteelop-ahrnah shay
bushpig	potamochère d'Afrique	potahmoshare-dafreek
caracal	caracal	kahrahkahl
cheetah	guépard	gu-epahr
chimpanzee	chimpanzé	shamponzay
civet	civette	see vet
colobus, black & white	colobe guereza	kolob guerezah
dikdik, Kirk's	dikdik de Kirk	deek deek duh kirk
duiker, common or grey	cephalophe du Cap	sefahlof du kap
eland	élan	aylon
elephant	elephant d'Afrique	aylayfon-dafreek
fox, bat-eared	otocyon	otoseeon
gazelle, Grant's	gazelle de Grant	gahzel duh grant
gazelle, Thomson's	gazelle de Thomson	gahzel duh tomson
gemsbok	oryx	oreex
genet, large spotted	genette à grandes taches	juhnet-ah-grand-tash
gerenuk	gazelle giraffe	gahzel giraf
giraffe	giraffe	giraf

MAMMAL NAMES

English	French	Phonetics
gorilla	gorille	goreeyuh
grysbok, Sharpe's	grysbok	greesbok
hare, scrub	lièvre des buissons	lee-evr de bueessan
hartebeest, red	bubale	bubal
hedgehog	hérisson du cap	ayreessan du kap
hippopotamus	hippoptame	eepopotahm
hog, giant forest	hylochère géant	ee-lo-share gayan
honey badger	ratel	rahtel
hyena, brown	hyène brune	yen brun
hyena, spotted	hyène tachetée	yen ta shuhte
hyena, striped	hyène rayée	yen re ye
hyrax, tree	daman d'arbre	dahmon dahrbr
impala	pallah	pah lah
jackal, black-backed	chacal à chabraque	shah kahl-ah-shahbrak
jackal, side-striped	chacal à flancs rayé	shah kahl-ah-flon-ray-ye
klipspringer	oreotrague	orayo trah guh
kob, Uganda	cob de Buffon	kob duh bufon
kudu, greater	grand koudou	gran koo doo
lechwe, red	cobe lechwe	kobe lechwe
leopard	lèopard	lay opahr
lion	lion	leeown
meerkat	suricate	mangooz-fov
mongoose, banded	mangue rayée	mangooz-ray-ye
monkey, Syke's	cercopitheque	sare ko pee tek
monkey, vervet	grivet	gree vay
nyala	nyala	nee ah lah
oribi	ourébie	oo ray bee
otter, clawless	loutre à joues blanches	lootr-ah-jeur-blansh
pangolin, Temminck's	pangolin de Temminck	pangola-duh-taymeek
porcupine	porc-épique	pork-ay-peek
puku	puku	puku
reedbuck, common	redunca grande	ruhdunka grand
rhino, black	rhinocéros noir	reenosayros nwar
rhino, white	rhinocéros blanc	reenosayros blan
serval	serval	sair vahl
sitatunga	sitatunga	see tah tun gah
springbok	antidorcas	an tee dor kah
springhare	lièvre	leeevr
squirrel, tree	e'cureuil des bois	aykuroyl-de-bwa
steenbok	steenbok	steenbok
topi	damalisque	dah mah leesk
tsessebe	sassaby	sah sah bee
warthog	phacochère	fah ko share
waterbuck, common	cobe à croissant	kob-ah-krwasson
waterbuck, defassa	cobe defassa	kob-defahssah
wild dog	cynhyène	seen yen
wildebeest	gnou bleu	gnu-bluh
zebra, Burchell's	zèbre de steppe	zabr-duh-step
zebra, Grevy's	zèbre de Grévy	zabr-duh-grayvee
zorilla	zorille	zoreeyl

209

Safari Glossary

Safari Glossary

Ablution block: A building that contains showers, toilets and sinks, most often with separate facilities for men and women.

Adaptation: The ability, through structural or functional characteristics, to improve the survival rate of an animal or plant in a particular habitat.

Age (approx.): Mammals — (1) adult = eight years and older, (2) juvenile = three to eight years, (3) infant = zero to three years.

Arboreal: Living in trees.

Banda: A basic shelter or hut, often constructed of reeds, bamboo, grass, etc.

Boma: A place of shelter, a fortified place, enclosure, community (East Africa).

Browse: To feed on leaves.

Calving season: Period when young of a particular species are born. Not all species have calving seasons. Most calving seasons occur shortly after the rainy season commences. Calving seasons can also differ for the same species from one park or reserve to another.

Camp: Camping sites; also refers to lodging in chalets, bungalows or tents in a remote location.

Caravan: A trailer.

Carnivore: An animal that lives by consuming the flesh of other animals.

Carrion: Remains of dead animals.

Diurnal: Active during the day.

Endangered: Refers to an animal that is threatened with extinction.

Gestation: Duration of pregnancy.

Grazer: An animal that eats grass.

Habitat: An animal's or plant's surroundings that has everything it needs in order to live.

Habituated: An animal that has been introduced to and accepted the presence of human beings.

Herbivore: An animal that consumes plant matter for food.

Hide: A camouflaged structure from which one can view wildlife without being seen.

Kopje (pronounced kopee): Rock formations which protrude from the savannah, usually caused by wind erosion (southern Africa).

Koppie: Same as kopje (East Africa).

Kraal: Same as boma (southern Africa).

Mammal: Warm-blooded animal that produces milk for its young.

Midden: Usually an accumulation of dung in the same spot as a scent-marking behavior.

Nocturnal: Active during the night.

Omnivore: An animal that eats both plant and animal matter.

Pan: Hard-surfaced flatlands that collect water in the rainy season.

Predator: An animal that hunts and kills other animals for food.

Prey: An animal hunted by a predator for food.

Pride: A group or family of lions.

Rondavel: An African-style structure for accommodation.

Ruminant: Mammal with complex stomach which therefore chews the cud.

Rutting: Behavioral pattern exhibited by male of the species over a time period that mating is most prevalent, e.g., impala, wildebeest.

Savannah: Open grassy landscape with widely scattered trees.

Scavenger: An animal that lives off of carrion or the remains of animals killed by predators or dead from other causes.

Species: A group of plants or animals with specific characteristics in common, including the ability to reproduce among themselves.

Spoor: A track (i.e., footprint) or trail made by animals.

Symbiosis: An association of two different organisms in a relationship that may benefit one or both partners.

Tarmac: Asphalt-paved road.

Territory: The home range or domain which an animal may defend against intruders of the same or other species.

Toilet, long-drop: A permanent bush toilet or "outhouse" in which a toilet seat has been placed over a hole which is dug about 6 feet (2 m) deep.

Toilet, short-drop: A temporary bush toilet, usually a toilet tent used on mobile tented safaris in which a toilet seat is placed over a hole which has been dug about 3 feet (1 m) deep.

Tracking: Following and observing animal spoor by foot.

Tribe: A group of people united by traditional ties.

Troop: A group of apes or monkeys.

Ungulate: Hoofed animal.

Veld: Southern African term for open land.

Wallow: The art of keeping cool and wet, usually in a muddy pool (i.e., rhinoceros, buffalo and hippopotamus).

Illustrations and Descriptions of Mammals, Reptiles, Birds and Trees

Mammal

ILLUSTRATIONS AND DESCRIPTIONS

Chimpanzee *(Pan troglodytes)*

French: chimpanzé
Height: 42–48 inches (107–122 cm)
Weight: 88–110 pounds (40–55 kg)
Gestation: 7+ months
No. of young: 1
Longevity: 50+ years
Spoor length: 8–10 inches (20–25 cm)
Black-haired, tailless ape with large ears; arms longer than legs; diurnal. Highly intelligent and gregarious in complex family troops. Feeds primarily on fruit but also capable of killing small mammals (including monkeys) and uses grass stems to "fish" termites from underground nests.

Mountain Gorilla *(Gorilla gorilla)*

French: gorille
Height: 59–71 inches (150–180 cm)
Weight: 250–450 pounds (114–205 kg)
Gestation: 8–9 months
No. of young: 1
Longevity: 25–30 years
Spoor length: 9.5–14 inches (24–35 cm)
Knuckle print width: 5–6.75 inches (13–17 cm)
Huge black-haired, tailless ape with massive head, high crown and long strong arms; diurnal. Lives in a family troop led by a dominant "silverback" male. Almost wholly vegetarian, feeding on leaves, roots and tubers. Gravely threatened in the remaining habitats of Virunga volcanoes (shared by Uganda, Rwanda and Democratic Republic of the Congo) and Bwindi (Uganda).

Black & White Colobus or Guereza
(Colobus guereza)

French: colobe guereza
Head & body length: 21–30 inches (54–75 cm)
Tail length: 28–35 inches (70–90 cm)
Weight: 22–26 pounds (10–22 kg)
Gestation: 5+ months
No. of young: 1
Longevity: 24+ years
Spoor length: 2.3 inches (5.5 cm)
Black and white, long-haired monkey; has no thumb, diurnal. The only truly herbivorous monkey, the colobus feeds exclusively on leaves. Favors forest along riverbanks and acacia woodlands adjacent to lakes. Troops consist of related females and their offspring and one or more dominant males.

Chacma Baboon *(Papio ursinus)*

French: le chacma
Shoulder height: 20–24 inches (50–61 cm)
Weight: 55–66 pounds (25–30 kg)
Gestation: 6+ months
No. of young: 1
Longevity: 18+ years
Spoor length: 5.5–6.3 inches (14–16 cm)
Large and powerfully built with small ears and short-haired tail; arms longer than legs; diurnal. Lives in a well-organized troop of up to 150 with several dominant males. Feeds on tubers, fruit and vertebrates, including newborn antelope. The southern race is known as the chacma baboon, the Zambian as the yellow baboon and the East African as the olive baboon; they differ in the length and color of their coats.

Vervet Monkey *(Cercopithecus aethiops)*

French: grivet
Head & body length: 16–31 inches (40–80 cm)
Tail length: 22–30 inches (56–75 cm)
Weight: 5.5–17 pounds (2.5–8 kg)
Gestation: 7+ months
No. of young: 1
Longevity: 12+ years
Spoor length: 2.1–2.4 inches (5.5–6 cm)
Greyish-green body with a long tail; diurnal. Most common primate of woodland and savannah. Troops number from 10 to 30 or more. Often becomes tame around human settlements (including lodges and camps), where it can become a nuisance if fed. Diet consists of insects, fruit and nestling birds.

Syke's Monkey *(Cercopithecus mitis kolbi)*

French: cercopitheque
Head & body length: 17–26 inches (44–67 cm)
Tail length: 22–42 inches (55–109 cm)
Weight: 6.5–15.5 pounds (3–7 kg)
Gestation: 4–4.5 months
No. of young: 1
Longevity: 24 years
Spoor length: 16 inches (40 cm)
Dark monkey, with variably colored coat; limbs and tail usually black; pale brow is conspicuous. Favors more densely wooded habitats than the vervet, including evergreen forest of coastal strip and highlands. A single dominant male leads small troops.

Greater Bushbaby *(Galago crassicaudatus)*

French: galago à queue epaisse
Head & body length: 12–18 inches (30–45 cm)
Tail length: 11–20 inches (28–50 cm)
Weight: 2.3–3.5 pounds (1–1.6 kg)
Gestation: 4+ months
No. of young: 1–3
Longevity: 14+ years

Spoor length: 1.4 inches (3.5 cm)
Grey-brown furry body with bushy tail and large round eyes; nocturnal. The eerie wailing call — likened to that of a lost infant — is used as a means of contact between the pair and as a territorial advertisement to neighbors. Favors well-wooded habitats, often along rivers, where insects are the main prey.

Lesser Bushbaby
(Galago senegalensis/moholi)

French: galago du Senegal
Head & body length: 5–8 inches (13–21 cm)
Tail length: 10 inches (26 cm)
Weight: 7 ounces (200 g)
Gestation: 130 days
No. of young: 1 or 2
Longevity: 6 years
Spoor length: 1 inch (2.5 cm)
Tiny grey-brown primate with long fluffy tail; nocturnal. Bounds through trees with great agility, following scent-marked pathways. Feeds on resin of acacia trees and small insects. Females and offspring occupy a home range, while males have larger territories that incorporate the ranges of several females. Favored habitat is acacia woodland and thickets.

Lion *(Panthera leo)*

French: lion
Shoulder height: 30–40 inches (75–102 cm)
Weight: 275–440 pounds (125–200 kg)
Gestation: 3+ months
No. of young: 1–4
Longevity: 20+ years
Spoor longevity: 17+ years
Spoor length: 3.5 inches (9 cm)
Unmistakable tawny cat with males having distinctive mane; most active at night but often seen during day. The only truly social cat; occurs in prides of related females which are lorded over by one or more dominant males. Preys on large mammals up to the size of giraffe and buffalo.

Leopard *(Panthera pardus)*

French: leopard, panthère d'Afrique
Shoulder height: 20–28 inches (50–71 cm)
Weight: 110–175 pounds (50–80 kg)
Gestation: 3+ months
No. of young: 2–3
Longevity: 20+ years
Spoor length: 2.75–3.5 inches (7–9 cm)
Identified by groups of dark spots in the form of rosettes; mainly nocturnal. Solitary and secretive, the leopard preys on small to medium-sized antelope as well as warthog, rodents, birds, reptiles and even insects. Pairs come together only to mate.

Cheetah *(Acinonyx jubatus)*

French: guépard
Shoulder height: 28–30 inches (71–76 cm)
Weight: 90–139 pounds (41–63 kg)
Gestation: 3+ months
No. of young: 1–5
Longevity: 12+ years
Spoor length: 3.5 inches (9 cm)
Slender cat with round black spots; small head; diurnal. The fastest land mammal, the cheetah reaches speeds of over 62 miles (100 km) per hour in short chases after its favored prey of gazelles and other small antelope. Usually hunts in the middle of the day, when larger carnivores are inactive.

Caracal *(Caracal caracal)*

French: caracal
Shoulder height: 16–20 inches (41–50 cm)
Weight: 20–40 pounds (9–18 kg)
Gestation: 2+ months
No. of young: 2–4
Longevity: 11+ years
Spoor length: 2 inches (5 cm)
Rufous coat; pointed ears with tufts of black hair; solitary and mainly nocturnal. Powerful for its size, this lynx-like cat is able to overpower antelope up to the size of duiker but favors hares, hyrax and game birds. Favors hilly or rocky habitats.

Serval *(Leptailurus serval)*

French: serval
Shoulder height: 18–21 inches (46–54 cm)
Weight: 13–35 pounds (6–16 kg)
Gestation: 2+ months
No. of young: 1–4
Longevity: 12+ years
Spoor length: 1.5–1.75 inches (4–4.5 cm)
Yellowish to reddish-yellow coat with large black spots and short ringed tail; mainly nocturnal. Often associated with rank grass near water, the serval is an expert hunter of birds, which are often caught in a mid-air pounce. At first glance, resembles a small leopard or cheetah.

African Wild Cat *(Felis sylvestris)*

French: chat ganté
Head & body length: 17.5–28.5 inches (45–73 cm)
Weight: 6.5–14 pounds (3–6.5 kg)
Gestation: 56–69 days
No. of young: 2–6
Longevity: 10 years
Spoor length: 1.5 inches (4 cm)
Closely resembles domestic cat, but with markedly longer legs and distinctive orange back to the ears. Primarily nocturnal, but frequently active during late afternoons in cool periods. Solitary, it feeds mostly on rodents and ground birds. In areas close to human settlement, it hybridizes easily with domestic cat, and genetic purity is threatened in such areas.

Civet *(Civettictis civetta)*

French: civette
Shoulder height: 13–16 inches (34–40 cm)
Weight: 20–45 pounds (9–20 kg)
Gestation: 2+ months
No. of young: 1–4
Longevity: 12+ years
Spoor length: 2 inches (5 cm)

Grey with black vertical stripes and blotches and black dorsal mane; long-haired; nocturnal. Solitary, raccoon-like predator of small vertebrates including millipedes, which are toxic to other predators; also feeds on berries and fruit. Rarely climbs trees.

Large Spotted Genet *(Genetta tigrina)*

French: genette à grandes taches
Shoulder height: 6–7.5 inches (16–19 cm)
Weight: 2.2–6.6 pounds (1–3 kg)
Gestation: 2+ months
No. of young: 2–5
Longevity: 13+ years
Spoor length: 1.2 inches (3 cm)

Yellowish-grey to brownish body with elongated dark spots; long ringed tail; nocturnal. Spends most of its time in trees, but regularly forages on the ground. Captures roosting birds as well as rodents and insects. Solitary and secretive.

Spotted Hyena *(Crocuta crocuta)*

French: hyène tachetée
Shoulder height: 27–36 inches (69–92 cm)
Weight: 125–185 pounds (57–85 kg)
Gestation: 3+ months
No. of young: 1–4
Longevity: 25+ years
Spoor length: 3.5–4.3 inches (9–11 cm)

Body grey, tawny or reddish with oval dark spots; sloping back; mainly nocturnal. Commonly thought of as a scavenger, the hyena is also a highly efficient predator of animals up to the size of wildebeest and zebra. Occurs in clans of 10 to 40 and is able to dominate lions in some regions. The eerie whooping and laughing calls are among Africa's most evocative night sounds.

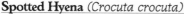

Brown Hyena *(Hyaena brunnea)*

French: hyène brune
Shoulder height: 28–31 inches (70–80 cm)
Weight: 100–120 pounds (45–55 kg)
Gestation: 3+ months
No. of young: 2–5
Longevity: 24+ years
Spoor length: 3–4 inches (8–10 cm)

Very shaggy dark brown coat with a light-colored mane and sloping back; several transverse black stripes on legs; nocturnal. A solitary scavenger restricted to the Namib and Kalahari deserts. Also feeds on wild cucumbers, reptiles and ground-nesting birds.

Striped Hyena *(Hyaena hyaena)*

French: hyène rayée
Shoulder height: 22–28 inches (55–80 cm)
Weight: 66–99 pounds (30–45 kg)
Gestation: 3 months
No. of young: 2–4
Longevity: 24+ years
Spoor length: 2.75–3.5 inches (7–9 cm)
Long-haired greyish body with black vertical stripes and bushy tail; nocturnal. Solitary scavenger of the drier parts of Kenya and Tanzania, where it often frequents the outskirts of rural villages.

Aardwolf *(Proteles cristatus)*

French: protèle
Shoulder height: 19 inches (50 cm)
Weight: 17–30 pounds (7.7–13.5 kg)
Gestation: 2+ months
No. of young: 2–4
Longevity: 13+ years
Spoor length: 2 inches (5 cm)
Yellow-brown to dull yellow with five or more distinct black stripes on the flanks and legs; nocturnal. Diminutive relative of the hyenas with a highly specialized diet of termites; tiny teeth are useless for killing or chewing larger prey.

Black-Backed Jackal *(Canis mesomelas)*

French: chacal à chabraque
Shoulder height: 16–20 inches (40–50 cm)
Weight: 13–22 pounds (6–10 kg)
Gestation: 2+ months
No. of young: 1–6
Longevity: 3+ years
Spoor length: 2 inches (5 cm)
Greyish-black back and yellowish-red sides and legs; bushy black-tipped tail; diurnal and nocturnal. African equivalent of the coyote; bold and wily, sometimes feeding alongside hyenas and even lions at carcasses. Plaintive wailing call is a characteristic night sound.

Golden Jackal *(Canis aureus)*

French: chacal commun
Head & body length: 26–41 inches (65–105 cm)
Weight: 13–33 pounds (6–15 kg)
Gestation: 2+ months
No. of young: 2–6
Longevity: 10 years
Spoor length: 2 inches (5 cm)
Overall sandy grey in color, with no distinctive stripes. Widespread in East and North Africa, even across the Sahara Desert. Where food is plentiful, several families may form group territories. It is common in the Serengeti-Mara and Ngorongoro Crater, where it often captures weak and young flamingos. Also joins other scavengers at carrion.

Side-Striped Jackal *(Canis adustus)*

French: chacal à flancs rayé
Shoulder height: 18–20 inches (46–50 cm)
Weight: 13–31 pounds (6–14 kg)
Gestation: 2–2.5 months
No. of young: 2–6
Longevity: 11+ years
Spoor length: 2 inches (5 cm)

Body greyish-brown or black with light longitudinal side stripe; diurnal and nocturnal. Least bold of the jackals and wary of approaching larger carnivores at carrion. Pairs defend a territory and feed on rodents, insects and reptiles.

Bat-Eared Fox *(Otocyon megalotis)*

French: otocyon
Shoulder height: 13–16 inches (33–40 cm)
Weight: 6.5–11 pounds (3–5 kg)
Gestation: 2+ months
No. of young: 2–6
Longevity: 12 years
Spoor length: 1.5 inches (4 cm)

Short greyish-brown body with long bushy tail and very large ears; nocturnal. Lives in family groups of four to eight and favors open grassy areas. Does not scavenge like jackals but unearths insects, reptiles and rodents, which are located by the huge radar-like ears.

Clawless Otter *(Aonyx capensis)*

French: loutre à joues blanches
Length: 51 inches (130 cm)
Weight: 22–40 pounds (10–18 kg)
Gestation: 9 weeks
No. of young: 1–2
Longevity: 15+ years
Spoor length: 3 inches (8 cm)

Dark color, with white throat, chin and upper chest; no claws on front feet; diurnal, sometimes nocturnal. Shy and secretive, the presence of this aquatic carnivore is usually only revealed by its paw prints in mud. Feeds primarily on fish and crabs.

Wild (Hunting) Dog *(Lycaon pictus)*

French: cynhyène
Shoulder height: 24–30 inches (60–76 cm)
Weight: 40–70 pounds (18–32 kg)
Gestation: 2–2.5 months
No. of young: 7–10
Longevity: 10+ years
Spoor length: 3.5 inches (9 cm)

Body blackish-brown or black with brownish-red, dark brown, yellow and white blotches; diurnal. Highly endangered pack-living predator with an advanced social system. Impala and other medium-sized antelope are run down and killed after a determined chase.

Honey Badger *(Mellivora capensis)*

French: ratel
Height: 10 inches (25 cm)
Weight: 18–33 pounds (8–15 kg)
Gestation: 6 months
No. of young: 2
Longevity: 16 years
Spoor length: 3 inches (8 cm)
Badger-like with silvery-grey saddle, jet black underbelly and white crown; diurnal or nocturnal. Very bold and powerful predator, known to stand its ground against much larger animals, including man. Excavates rodents and reptiles from underground burrows and may scavenge from campsites.

Zorilla *(Ictonyx striatus)*

French: zorille
Head & body length: 12–16 inches (30–40 cm)
Tail length: 8–10 inches (21–25 cm)
Weight: 2.2–6.5 pounds (1–3 kg)
Gestation: 5–6 weeks
No. of young: 1–3
Longevity: 8+ years
Spoor length: 1.5 inches (4 cm)
Black and white striped upper body and tail; long-haired with bushy tail; nocturnal. Solitary, secretive and very rarely seen. Close relative of the North American skunk.

Banded Mongoose *(Mungos mungo)*

French: mangue rayée
Height: 5 inches (12.5 cm)
Weight: 2.2–3.5 pounds (1–4 kg)
Gestation: 2 months
No. of young: 2–8
Longevity: 13 years
Spoor length: 1.5 inches (3.5 cm)
Distinct dark bands run across the back from the shoulders to the end of the tail; diurnal. Lives in packs of up to 40 members (usually smaller), with one dominant male and up to four breeding females. Forages in tightly bunched subgroups and known to come rapidly to the aid of any member threatened or captured by a predator.

Slender Mongoose *(Herpestes sanguinea)*

French: mangouste rouge
Head & body length: 10–13 inches (26–34 cm)
Weight: 0.75–1.75 pounds (350–800 g)
Gestation: 2 months
No. of young: 2 to 3
Longevity: 8 years
Spoor length: 1 inch (3 cm)
Solitary, long-tailed mongoose; diurnal. Variable in color, with southern races rusty red with a distinctive black-tipped tail and those in East Africa often chocolate brown to black. Feeds on birds, rodents and insects, sometimes by climbing low trees. In common with other mongooses, quite willing to attack and kill venomous snakes.

Dwarf Mongoose *(Helogale parvula)*

French: mangouste nain
Head & body length: 7–9 inches (18–24 cm)
Weight: 0.5–0.7 pound (210–320 g)
Gestation: 53 days
Longevity: 8 years
Spoor length: 1 inch (2.5 cm)

Tiny, greyish-coated mongoose with pink snout; diurnal. Very gregarious in troops averaging eight (but up to 20) with a single dominant female as the leader. Invariably associated with termite mounds in which the troop retreats at danger, sleeps and raises young. Has a mutually beneficial relationship with hornbills, which alert the mongoose to danger (hawks and eagles) and benefit from the capture of disturbed insects.

Meerkat *(Suricata suricata)*

French: suricate
Head & body length: 10–20 inches (25–30 cm)
Weight: 1.3–2.1 pounds (620–960 g)
Gestation: 10–11 weeks
No. of young: 2–5
Longevity: 12+ years
Spoor length: 1 inch (3 cm)

Silver-brown to slightly paler with dark spots on back, dark tail and dark area around eyes; diurnal. Highly sociable member of the mongoose family, restricted to the Kalahari, Karoo and Namib. Packs of up to ten vigorously defend their territories from rivals. When foraging for lizards, beetles and other insects, at least one of the pack stands as a lookout for eagles and large hawks.

Temminck's Ground Pangolin
(Smutsia temmincki)

French: pangolin de Temminck
Head & body length: 14–27 inches (35–60 cm)
Weight: 15–20 pounds (7–9 kg)
Gestation: 4–5 months
No. of young: 1
Longevity: 12+ years
Spoor length: 1.5–2.4 inches (4–6 cm)

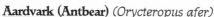

Covered with light brown scales that average 1.5 inches (4 cm) in width; nocturnal. Specialized scaly anteater able to roll itself into a tight ball when threatened. The long sticky tongue is used to lick up vast quantities of ants and termites during nocturnal foraging bouts.

Aardvark (Antbear) *(Orycteropus afer)*

French: fourmillier, oryctérope
Shoulder height: 16–26 inches (40–65 cm)
Weight: 110–150 pounds (50–68 kg)
Gestation: 7+ months
No. of young: 1
Longevity: 10+ years
Spoor length: 2.75–3.5 inches (7–9 cm)

Pale brown body with elongated snout, big ears, long tongue and long heavy tail; nocturnal. Specialized ant- and termite-eater with incredibly powerful forelimbs and claws that enable it to excavate in solid ground. Shy and seldom seen, with an acute sense of hearing. Aardvark burrows are often usurped by hyena, warthog and other creatures.

African Porcupine *(Hystrix africae-australis)*
French: porc-épique
Head & body length: 26–33 inches (65–85 cm)
Tail length: 4.75–7 inches (12–17 cm)
Weight: 33–55 pounds (15–25 kg)
Gestation: 3 months
No. of young: 1–4
Longevity: 8+ years
Spoor length:
Hind foot: 3–3.5 inches (8–9 cm)
Forefoot: 2–2.4 inches (5–6 cm)
Long black and white quills; nocturnal. Africa's largest rodent which, despite its dangerous quills, is preyed upon by lion and leopard. Lives in pairs with offspring, returning to a favored burrow after a night of foraging. Distinctive ring-barking of favored trees often betrays its presence in an area. Not able to "shoot" quills as sometimes described.

Hedgehog *(Atelerix frontalis)*
French: hérisson du cap
Head & body length: 6–10 inches (15–25 cm)
Weight: 9–54 ounces (250–1500 g)
Gestation: 5 weeks
No. of young: 1–9
Longevity: 3+ years
Spoor length: 0.75 inch (1.5–2 cm)
Body covered with short small spines; face framed with white hair across the forehead; nocturnal. Forages alone or in family groups in search of earthworms and insects. Spends the day in an underground burrow. Very rarely seen but frequently preyed upon, in some areas, by giant eagle owl.

Scrub Hare *(Lepus saxtilis)*
French: lièvre des buissons
Head & body length: 16–22 inches (40–55 cm)
Weight: 3–10 pounds (1.5–4.4 kg)
Gestation: 5+ weeks
No. of young: 1–3
Longevity: 7+ years
Spoor length: 1.25 inches (3.2 cm)
A dull yellow with black-grey speckles; tail black on top, white underneath; nocturnal, appearing at sunset. Sometimes flushed during the day by large mammals or off-road vehicles, running off in a zigzag fashion. Cheetah actively pursues flushed hares, as do larger eagles. Young are born above ground and develop quickly.

Springhare *(Pedetes capensis)*
French: lièvre
Head & body length: 14–16 inches (35–40 cm)
Weight: 5–8 pounds (2.5–3.8 kg)
Gestation: 3 months
No. of young: 1

Longevity: 6 years
Spoor length: 1.25 inches (3.2 cm)
Has the action and appearance of a very small kangaroo; extremely long and powerful hind legs; nocturnal. Occurs in colonies in open areas of compressed sandy soil. Remains in underground burrow during the day. Easily detected with flashlight after dark. Preyed upon by eagle owls, caracal and leopard.

Ground Squirrel *(Geosciurus inaurus)*
French: écureuil foisseur
Head & body length: 8–12 inches (20–30 cm)
Tail length: 8 inches (20 cm)
Weight: 1–2 pounds (500 to 1000 g)
Gestation: 2 months
No. of young: 1 to 3
Longevity: 8 years
Spoor length: 1.3 inches (3.5 cm)
Sand-colored squirrel which forages on the ground and dwells in an underground burrow; diurnal. Restricted to the Kalahari, Karoo and Namib, but the very similar striped ground squirrel occurs in parts of East Africa. Feeds on roots, seeds and acacia pods. In treeless areas, this squirrel has the fascinating habit of facing away from the sun and using its upheld tail as a shade umbrella.

Tree Squirrel (Smith's Bush Squirrel)
(Paraxerus cepapi)
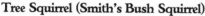
French: L'ecureuil des bois
Head & body length: 5.5–7 inches (14–18 cm)
Weight: 35 ounces (150 g)
Gestation: 2 months
No. of young: 1–3
Longevity: 8+ years
Spoor length: 0.9 inch (2.3 cm)
Small, buffy speckled grey with lighter underbelly; long tail is bushy; diurnal. Spends most of its time in trees. Utters a persistent chirping call when danger threatens and guides may use this call as a clue to the whereabouts of leopard.

African Elephant *(Loxodonta africana)*

French: elephant d'Afrique
Shoulder height: 8–11 feet (3–3.4 m)
Weight: 8800–13,750 pounds (4000–6250 kg)
Gestation: 22 months
No. of young: 1
Longevity: 65+ years
Spoor length: up to 31 inches (80 cm)
Very large ears; smooth forehead; large, curved tusks; diurnal and nocturnal. Bulk feeder on grass, leaves, twigs, bark, roots and fruit; the bush-bashing habits of the elephant have a profound effect on vegetation structure in various habitats. Consumes up to 660 pounds (300 kg) of food per day and drinks daily, sometimes digging wells in dry riverbeds.

Rock Hyrax *(Procavia capensis)*

French: daman de rocher
Head & body length: 16–23.5 inches (40–60 cm)
Weight: 4.4–11 pounds (2.0 to 5 kg)
Gestation: 8 months
No. of young: 1 to 6
Longevity: 20 years
Spoor length: 1.5 inches (4 cm)
Distantly related to the elephant and manatee, with internal testes and blunt "hoofed" digits. Lives on rocky outcrops and mountain slopes; diurnal. Often seen sunning themselves in early morning. Males hold territories, containing up to 20 or more females. Adjacent groups may form large colonies. Feeds on leaves, grass and berries. Favored prey of Verreaux's (black) eagle and also taken by leopard.

Tree Hyrax *(Dendrohyrax arboreus)*

French: daman d'arbre
Head & body length: 14–23 inches (35–60 cm)
Weight: 4.4–10 pounds (2.0–4.5 kg)
Gestation: 8 months
No. of young: 1–3
Longevity: 20 years
Spoor length: 1.5 inches (4 cm)
Grey to brown fur with white patch of hair in middle of back; mainly arboreal and nocturnal. The astonishing nocturnal calls of the tree hyrax can be rather terrifying to the uninitiated. Males shriek and scream at one another, setting off all surrounding territory holders. Browses on the leaves of acacias and other trees.

Cape Buffalo *(Syncerus caffer)*

French: buffle d'Afrique
Shoulder height: 43–65 inches (110–165 cm)
Weight: 880–1760 pounds (400–800 kg)
Gestation: 11 months
No. of young: 1
Longevity: 23+ years
Spoor length: 4.75–6.3 inches (12–16 cm)
Massive; blackish in color with widely curved, thick horns; diurnal and nocturnal. Highly gregarious bulk grazer in herds of up to 1000, which consist of numerous family clusters. Older bulls live alone in small bachelor groups and can be extremely dangerous. Drinks daily and retreats to thickets and forests after dark.

Hippopotamus *(Hippopotamus amphibius)*

French: hippopotame
Shoulder height: 55–63 inches (140–160 cm)
Weight: 990–7260 pounds (450–3300 kg)
Gestation 7.5–8 months
No. of young: 1
Longevity: 39+ years
Spoor length: 8–10 inches (20–25 cm)
Pinkish brown skin with enormous head and four large curved tusks; rests in water by day, grazes at night. Occurs in "pods" of between 6 and 150, with much vocalizing in response to disturbances and to maintain hierarchy among males. Competing males may engage in fierce, bloody fights.

White Rhino *(Ceratotherium simum)*

French: rhinocéros blanc
Shoulder height: 69–81 inches (175–205 cm)
Weight: 6600–8800 pounds (3000–4000 kg)
Gestation: 16 months
No. of young: 1
Longevity: 45+ years
Spoor length: 8–11 inches (21–28 cm)

Square mouth with very wide upper lip; long-headed with hump in front of shoulder; diurnal and nocturnal. Feeds exclusively on grass. Where common (several South African reserves), up to 16 may gather together to feed, but usually found singly or as a mother and calf. Immune to most predators, but young vulnerable to lion and spotted hyena.

Black Rhino *(Diceros bicornis)*

French: rhinocéros noir
Shoulder height: 55–67 inches (140–170 cm)
Weight: 1760–3520 pounds (800–1600 kg)
Gestation: 15 months
No. of young: 1
Longevity: 40+ years
Spoor length: 8–10 inches (20–25 cm)

Grey body with pointed prehensile upper lip; no hump in front of shoulder; diurnal and nocturnal. Feeds exclusively on leaves and shoots of trees and shrubs (not grass). Solitary or in small groups. Has a reputation as a highly aggressive animal, particularly in densely bushed habitats. Immune to most predators, but young vulnerable to lion and spotted hyena.

Burchell's Zebra *(Equus burchelli)*

French: zèbre de steppe, zèbre de Burchell
Shoulder height: 47–55 inches (120–140 cm)
Weight: 495–770 pounds (225–350 kg)
Gestation: 12 months
No. of young: 1
Longevity: 35+ years
Spoor length: 4–4.3 inches (10–11 cm)

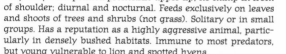

Almost pure black and white stripes; legs with stripes to the hoofs; diurnal and nocturnal. Widespread from Sudan to South Africa, with several races distinguished by the pattern of stripes; southern animals have distinctive "shadow" stripes. Feeds exclusively on grass; many populations are migratory and undertake seasonal movements with wildebeest.

Grevy's Zebra *(Equus grevyi)*

French: zèbre de Grévy
Shoulder height: 55–61 inches (140–155 cm)
Weight: 660–935 pounds (300–425 kg)
Gestation: 12+ months
No. of young: 1
Longevity: 21+ years
Spoor length: 4.3–4.75 inches (11–12 cm)

White body with closely set black or dark brown narrow vertical stripes; belly white without stripes; diurnal. Restricted to semi-arid parts of central and northern Kenya and Ethiopia. Feeds exclusively on grass, often associating with antelope and giraffe.

Bushpig *(Potamochoerus porcus)*

French: potamochère d'Afrique
Shoulder height: 22–31 inches (55–80 cm)
Weight: 100–300 pounds (45–136 kg)
Gestation: 4+ months
No. of young: 3–8
Longevity: 20+ years
Spoor length: 2.4 inches (6 cm)
Grey-brown to reddish-brown with short tusks, long ear tufts and light-colored dorsal mane; nocturnal. Widespread and common in certain habitats, but very rarely seen. Omnivorous, but feeds mostly on roots and tubers which are dug up with the pointed snout and sharp trotters. Also known to scavenge from carrion.

Giant Forest Hog
(Hylochoerus meinertzhageni)

French: hylochère géant
Shoulder height: 30–39 inches (75–100 cm)
Weight: 200–550 pounds (90–250 kg)
Gestation: 4–4.5 months
No. of young: 1–4
Longevity: 20+ years
Spoor length: 2.75 inches (7 cm)
Large thick body with coarse black hair and well-developed tusks; mainly nocturnal. The world's largest member of the pig family. Very rarely encountered except at Queen Elizabeth National Park (Uganda) and the Aberdares (Kenya). Feeds on grass and herbs, digging much less than bushpig or warthog.

Warthog *(Phacochoerus aethiopicus)*

French: phacochère
Shoulder height: 28–33 inches (70–85 cm)
Weight: 132–308 pounds (60–140 kg)
Gestation: 5.5 months
No. of young: 1–8
Longevity: 20+ years
Spoor length: 2 inches (5 cm)
Grey skin with bristly mane and shoulders; long upper tusks; large wart-like growths in front of eyes; diurnal. Lives in family group of females and their offspring. Feeds primarily on grass, going down on the knees to graze. Heavily preyed upon by lion and leopard. When on the run, the upheld tail is distinctive and gives this pig a comical appearance.

Giraffe (*Giraffa camelopardalis*)

French: giraffe
Height: 11.5–17 feet (3.5–5.2 m)
Weight: 2200–4180 pounds (1000 to 1900 kg)
Gestation: 14–15 months
No. of young: 1
Longevity: 28+ years
Spoor length: 7.5 inches (19 cm)

The world's tallest mammal and uniquely adapted to browse on savannah trees, particularly acacias. Diurnal and usually seen in small groups, although these gatherings are temporary. Several subspecies are recognized on the basis of their coat pattern and arrangement of "horns." Young are heavily preyed upon by lion and spotted hyena, with less than half surviving their first year. Rival males often engage in "necking," which is a form of dominance. Often attended by oxpeckers, which remove ticks from the coat and ears.

Rothschild's Giraffe
(*Giraffa camelopardalis rothschildi*)

Thickset body with yellowish-brown blotchy, rounded markings.

Reticulated Giraffe
(*Giraffa camelopardalis reticulata*)

Liver-red body marked with a network of white lines mostly quadrangular in shape.

Masai Giraffe
(*Giraffa camelopardalis tippelskirchi*)

Body yellowish with pale or dark jagged-edged almost star-like markings.

Sable Antelope *(Hippotragus niger)*

French: hippotrague noir
Shoulder height: 43–65 inches (110–165 cm)
Weight: 395–550 pounds (180–250 kg)
Gestation: 9 months
No. of young: 1
Longevity: up to 19 years
Spoor length: 3.5–4 inches (9–10 cm)
Male is jet black in color, with impressive rapier-like horns, while the female is rusty brown with shorter horns. Herds number up to 100 in ideal habitats, but are generally much smaller, with a single dominant bull.

Roan Antelope *(Hippotragus equinus)*

French: hippotrague, rouanne
Shoulder height: 55–63 inches (140–160 cm)
Weight: 550–600 pounds (250–273 kg)
Gestation: 9–9.5 months
No. of young: 1
Longevity: 19+ years
Spoor length: 4–4.3 inches (10–11 cm)
Upper side of body light brown to grey; distinctive black and white facial markings; diurnal. Robust, grazer of medium-tall grasses. Herds number between 5 and 35, with a single dominant bull, and may remain in a favored home range for months on end. Favors park-like savannah where other herbivores are scarce.

Gemsbok or Oryx *(Oryx gazella)*

French: oryx
Shoulder height: 43–55 inches (110–140 cm)
Weight: 395–485 pounds (180–220 kg)
Gestation: 9+ months
No. of young: 1
Longevity: 19+ years
Spoor length: 4.3–4.75 inches (11–12 cm)
Pale grey upper body with black and white markings on the face; mainly diurnal. Impressive arid-adapted antelope with scimitar-like horns. Primarily a grazer but will turn to leaves in the absence of grass and frequently digs up moisture-rich tubers. Lion and other predators show great respect for the dangerous horns.

Impala *(Aepyceros melampus)*

French: pallah
Shoulder height: 31–41 inches (80–105 cm)
Weight: 97–175 pounds (44–80 kg)
Gestation: 6.5 months
No. of young: 1
Longevity: 12+ years
Spoor length: 1.5–2 inches (4–5 cm)

Brownish body; buttocks white with black streaks; white
abdomen; diurnal. As both a grazer of grass and a browser of
leaves (most other antelope are one or the other), the impala
is frequently the most common antelope in open woodlands
and bush country. Only the male has the lyre-shaped horns
(which are much longer in East African populations). Herds
of 100 or more are lorded over by a single dominant ram.

Eland *(Taurotragus oryx)*

French: élan
Shoulder height: 55–71 inches (140–180 cm)
Weight: 880–1800 pounds (400–817 kg)
Gestation: 9 months
No. of young: 1
Longevity: 12+ years
Spoor length: 4.3–5.5 inches (11–14 cm)

Body greyish-brown to reddish-brown; thick spiraled horns;
mainly diurnal. Africa's largest antelope. Browses on the
leaves of various trees and the seed pods of acacias. Occurs in
small herds, sometimes with other antelope or zebra. Despite
its huge size is able to clear heights of over 5 feet (1.5 m).

Greater Kudu *(Tragelaphus strepsiceros)*

French: grand koudou
Shoulder height: 53–59 inches (135–150 cm)
Weight: 550–693 pounds (250–315 kg)
Gestation: 7 months
No. of young: 1
Longevity: 14+ years
Spoor length: 3–3.5 inches (8–9 cm)

Greyish-brown or fawn in color with several narrow white
vertical stripes on the side; diurnal and nocturnal. The magnificent spiral horns of the male make this one of the most
impressive antelope. A dedicated browser of *Combretum*,
Acacia and other leaves. Favors bushy habitats, where the
striped coat provides excellent camouflage.

Bongo *(Tragelaphus eurycerus)*

French: bongo
Shoulder height: 43–51 inches (110–130 cm)
Weight: 495–595 pounds (225–270 kg)
Gestation: 9.5 months
No. of young: 1
Longevity: up to 19 years
Spoor length: 3.5–4 inches (9–10 cm)

Body dark brown or chestnut with vertical white stripes;
diurnal and nocturnal. Secretive, forest-dwelling antelope.
Striped coat provides wonderful camouflage.

Sitatunga *(Tragelaphus spekei)*

French: sitatunga
Shoulder height: 35–47 inches (90–120 cm)
Weight: 155–253 pounds (70–115 kg)
Gestation: 7+ months
No. of young: 1
Longevity: 19+ years
Spoor length: 2.75 inches (7 cm)
Aquatic antelope; greyish brown to brown shaggy coat; mainly diurnal. Occurs singly or in pairs in dense papyrus swamps, feeding primarily on aquatic plants as well as short grass and sedges. Good but slow swimmer, although vulnerable to attack by crocodiles.

Bushbuck *(Tragelaphus scriptus)*

French: antilope harnaché, guib
Shoulder height: 27–39 inches (69–100 cm)
Weight: 77–185 pounds (35–80 kg)
Gestation: 6 months
No. of young: 1
Longevity: 11+ years
Spoor length: 1.5–2.4 inches (4–6 cm)
Brown body, may have vertical stripes and/or white spots; mainly nocturnal. Often found in the company of baboons, which serve to warn it of danger and provide food in the form of fallen fruit and leaves. The horned male is courageous and puts up a spirited defense when attacked. Coat color and pattern of stripes and spots vary from region to region.

Nyala *(Tragelaphus angasi)*

French: nyala
Shoulder height: 38–47 inches (95–120 cm)
Weight: 220–308 pounds (100–140 kg)
Gestation: 7 months
No. of young: 1
Longevity: 13+ years
Spoor length: 2–2.4 inches (5–6 cm)
Long shaggy coat; large ears; numerous white vertical stripes on side; diurnal and nocturnal. Female is completely different from male, with short, fawn-colored coat and no horns. Feeds on leaves as well as grass.

Red Lechwe *(Kobus leche)*

French: cob lechwe
Shoulder height: 35–43 inches (90–110 cm)
Weight: 198–285 pounds (90–130 kg)
Gestation: 7–8 months
No. of young: 1
Longevity: 15 years
Spoor length: 2.75–3 inches (7–8 cm)
Yellowish-brown upper body; elevated rump; fairly long coat; diurnal. Elegant marsh-loving antelope which favors margins between swamps and floodplains. Adapted to run through shallow water with splayed hooves. Confined to the Okavango Delta and swamplands of Zambia.

Uganda Kob *(Kobus kob)*

French: cob de buffon
Shoulder height: 62.5–70 inches (160–180 cm)
Weight: 132–264 pounds (60–120 kg)
Gestation: 8 months
No. of young: 1
Longevity: 12-15 years
Spoor length: 3 inches (8 cm)

Medium-sized antelope; male has thick, lyre-shaped horns; coat is a rich sandy red with black to the front of limbs. Occurs in family groups or herds of up to 200; males defend small territories into which females are herded. Dependent on drinking water and favors shortgrass areas close to lakes and rivers. In East Africa, now restricted to Uganda, where abundant in certain reserves.

Puku *(Kobus vardoni)*

French: puku
Shoulder height: 39 inches (100 cm)
Weight: 110–200 pounds (50–90 kg)
Gestation: 8 months
No. of young: 1
Longevity: 12 years
Spoor length: 2.7 inches (7 cm)

Like lechwe but smaller; reddish or gold-brown and ears fringed with black; short tail; active at sunrise or sunset. Smaller, stocky relative of the lechwe, and sometimes regarded as a southern race of the Uganda kob. Occurs in herds of 50 or more on floodplains and adjacent grassy woodlands.

Defassa Waterbuck *(Kobus defassa)*

French: cobe defassa
Shoulder height: 43–55 inches (110–135 cm)
Weight: 385–550 pounds (175–250 kg)
Gestation: 9 months
No. of young: 1
Longevity: 14+ years
Spoor length: 3.5 inches (9 cm)

Brown to grey-brown with double white patch on buttocks; ringed horns; diurnal. Considered by some authorities to be a race of the common waterbuck. Feeds primarily on grasses and sedges, but may browse on fresh leaves. Never far from water and will often swim into pools or rivers when pursued by predators.

Common Waterbuck *(Kobus ellipsiprymnus)*

French: cobe à croissant
Shoulder height: 43–55 inches (110–135 cm)
Weight: 385–550 pounds (175–250 kg)
Gestation: 9 months
No. of young: 1
Longevity: 14+ years
Spoor length: 3.5 inches (9 cm)

Grey-brown with white ring around buttocks; ringed horns; diurnal. Lives in small herds of up to 12 or so, but temporary aggregations may occur in optimum habitats. Family herd is faithful to defended home range for many years. Only the male possesses horns.

Common Reedbuck *(Redunca arundinum)*

French: redunca grande
Shoulder height: 31–39 inches (80–100 cm)
Weight: 132–220 pounds (60–100 kg)
Gestation: 7.5–8 months
No. of young: 1
Longevity: 9+ years
Spoor length: 2.4 inches (6 cm)
Body greyish-brown to dark brown; horns curved forward; diurnal and nocturnal. Occurs solitarily, in pairs or in small groups in marshes and wetlands. Usually wary and seldom seen, the reedbuck has a sharp whistle-like call.

Common or Grey Duiker *(Sylvicapra grimmia)*

French: cephalophe du cap
Shoulder height: 16–25 inches (40–63 cm)
Weight: 26–40 pounds (12–18 kg)
Gestation: 3 months
No. of young: 1
Longevity: 12 years
Spoor length: 1.2–1.4 inches (3–3.5 cm)
Fawn to greyish-brown body; dark stripe down middle of face; mainly nocturnal. Occurs in pairs, which often forage some distance apart in a home range. Feeds on leaves, shoots and fallen berries. Favors well-wooded habitats, where leopard is its main predator.

Red Duiker *(Cephalophus natalensis)*

French: cephalophe de Natal
Height: 29–34 inches (75–87 cm)
Weight: 26.5–31 pounds (12–14 kg)
Gestation: 5–6 months
Longevity: 10 years
Spoor length: 1.5 inches (4 cm)
Small, rust red antelope with short horns almost hidden by tuft of hair between ears; diurnal and nocturnal. Lives in pairs, which forage apart in dense habitats such as thicket and forest. Feeds on fallen leaves and berries. Principal enemies are leopard and crowned eagle. Occurs in coastal areas from South Africa to southern Tanzania. The very similar Peter's and Harvey's duiker occur in forested habitats in East Africa.

Suni *(Neotragus moschatus)*

French: antilope musquée
Height: 22–24 inches (57–62 cm)
Weight: 9–13 pounds (4–6 kg)
Gestation: 6 months
Longevity: 8 years
Spoor length: 1 inch (2.5 cm)
Tiny, tawny-colored antelope of forests and thickets; mostly nocturnal. Male possesses slim pointed horns. Browses on a variety of leaves and sometimes fungi. Pairs occupy territories which are constantly marked with dropping middens. The tail is distinctively marked in black and white and is constantly wagged from side to side. Vulnerable to most nocturnal predators and large eagles when active during the day.

Kirk's Dikdik *(Madoqua kirkii)*

French: dikdik de Kirk
Shoulder height: 12–18 inches (36–45 cm)
Weight: 6–14 pounds (2.8–6.5 kg)
Gestation: 6 months
No. of young: 1
Longevity: 6+ years
Spoor length: 0.75 inch (2 cm)

Greyish body with white belly; long nose; diurnal. Tiny arid-adapted antelope in two distinct populations. The southern race is confined to the Namib and adjacent scrub country and the northern race to acacia-dominated drylands. Completely independent of drinking water, the tube-like nostrils serve as a cooling mechanism. Lives in pairs, often with their most recent offspring.

Steenbok *(Raphicerus campestris)*

French: steenbok
Shoulder height: 20–24 inches (50–60 cm)
Weight: 26–35 pounds (12–16 kg)
Gestation: 6 months
No. of young: 1
Longevity: 6+ years
Spoor length: 1 inch (2.5 cm)

Reddish-brown to grey body with very large ears; diurnal. Mixed feeder of grass, leaves, seed pods and berries. Lives in pairs in a home range, favoring open habitats. Preyed upon by cheetah, leopard and martial eagle.

Sharpe's Grysbok *(Raphicerus melanotis)*

French: grysbok
Height: 17–19 inches (45–50 cm)
Weight: 14–25 pounds (6.4–11.3 kg)
Gestation: 7+ months
No. of young: 1
Longevity: 10 years
Spoor length: 1 inch (2.5 cm)

Light brown around the neck and reddish brown with white speckles on the body; horns very short; usually nocturnal. Shy and seldom seen, the grysbok favors thickets and the bases of rocky outcrops. Browses on leaves and buds and also feeds on berries as well as grass. Leopard and larger eagles are the main predators.

Oribi *(Ourebia ourebi)*

French: ourébie
Shoulder height: 20–26 inches (51–67 cm)
Weight: 31–48 pounds (14–22 kg)
Gestation: 7 months
No. of young: 1
Longevity: 13+ years
Spoor length: 1.2 inches (3 cm)

Fawn-grey to rufous body with dark spot at base of ear; mainly diurnal. Occurs in pairs or small family groups in open grassy habitats of hilltops or floodplains. Particularly fond of recently burned and heavily trampled areas. Cheetah and leopard are its principal predators.

Klipspringer *(Oreotragus oreotragus)*

French: oreotrague
Shoulder height: 18–24 inches (47–61 cm)
Weight: 22–42 pounds (10–19 kg)
Gestation: 7–7.5 months
No. of young: 1
Longevity: 7+ years
Spoor length: 1.2 inches (3 cm)
Thick yellowish or brownish body with rounded back and short tail; mainly diurnal. Specially adapted, cushion-like hooves allow the klipspringer to live among rocks and boulders, jumping with great agility in the manner of a mountain goat. Pairs live in territories with their most recent offspring.

Wildebeest or Gnu *(Connochaetes taurinus)*

French: gnou bleu
Shoulder height: 49–56 inches (125–143 cm)
Weight: 385–615 pounds (175–280 kg)
Gestation: 8.5 months
No. of young: 1
Longevity: 20+ years
Spoor length: 4 inches (10 cm)
Brown or grey body with humped back; mane and tail black; slender legs; diurnal. The Serengeti–Mara population, estimated at 1.5 million, is well known for its dramatic annual migration. Young are able to run with herd within hours of birth. Favored prey of lion and spotted hyena.

Topi *(Damaliscus korrigum)*

French: damalisque
Shoulder height: 47–51 inches (120–130 cm)
Weight: 285–320 pounds (130–145 kg)
Gestation: 7.5–8 months
No. of young: 1
Longevity: 12+ years
Spoor length: 2.75–3 inches (7–8 cm)
Body purplish-brown; very similar to the tsessebe; diurnal. Topi male typically stands atop termite mound to advertise its position and dominance. Favors seasonally flooded grasslands, where it feeds selectively on certain grasses. Large numbers engage in migratory movements in Tanzania and Kenya.

Tsessebe *(Damaliscus lunatus)*

French: sassaby
Shoulder height: 47–51 inches (120–130 cm)
Weight: 285–320 pounds (130–145 kg)
Gestation: 8 months
No. of young: 1
Longevity: 15+ years
Spoor length: 2.75–3 inches (7–8 cm)
Brownish or reddish body with dark patches on the shoulders and thighs; mainly diurnal. Considered by some authorities to be the southern race of the topi, this is a more slender antelope of the Okavango Delta, Zimbabwe woodlands and Kruger National Park.

Red Hartebeest *(Alcelaphus buselaphus)*

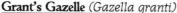

French: bubale
Shoulder height: 47–55 inches (120–140 cm)
Weight: 285–460 pounds (130–210 kg)
Gestation: 8+ months
No. of young: 1
Longevity: 13+ years
Spoor length: 4.3–4.7 inches (11–12 cm)
Brownish body with lighter colored rump; narrow head and humped shoulder; diurnal. Two populations occur: the red hartebeest in the Kalahari and Karoo–Namib fringe of southern Africa and the Kongoni in East Africa. A grazer of shortgrasses. Along with topi and tsessebe, this is one of the fastest of antelope.

Grant's Gazelle *(Gazella granti)*

French: gazelle de Grant
Shoulder height: 31–39 inches (80–100 cm)
Weight: 100–176 pounds (45–80 kg)
Gestation: 6.5 months
No. of young: 1
Longevity: 14+ years
Spoor length: 1.5–2 inches (4–5–cm)
Sandy-rufous upper body with white belly; black vertical stripe on outer edge of white buttocks; diurnal. The larger of the two common gazelles in East Africa and much paler in color than Thomson's gazelle. Favors areas of very short grass, and independent of drinking water.

Thomson's Gazelle *(Gazella thomsoni)*

French: gazelle de Thomson
Shoulder height: 24–29 inches (60–70 cm)
Weight: 48–60 pounds (22–27 kg)
Gestation: 6 months
No. of young: 1
Longevity: 10+ years
Spoor length: 1.5 inches (5 cm)
Rufous upper body with black lateral stripe above white belly; diurnal. This small, energetic gazelle occurs in small family groups or large herds which migrate behind the massive herds of wildebeest. Favors areas of shortgrass. Preyed upon by cheetah and leopard; the young are vulnerable to hyenas, jackals and eagles.

Springbok *(Antidorcas marsupialis)*

French: antidorcas
Shoulder height: 30–35 inches (76–90 cm)
Weight: 55–120 pounds (25–50 kg)
Gestation: 6+ months
No. of young: 1
Longevity: 10+ years
Spoor length: 2 inches (5 cm)
Brownish upper body with broad dark brown stripe along flank; white belly; diurnal. Adapted to the arid ecosystems of the Kalahari, Karoo and Namib of southern Africa. Its name is derived from its habit of "pronking" in spring-like bounds. Occurs in herds of several hundred or more and formerly undertook large-scale migrations across Botswana and South Africa.

239

Gerenuk *(Litocranius walleri)*

French: gazelle de Waller, gazelle giraffe
Shoulder height: 35–41 inches (90–105 cm)
Weight: 77–120 pounds (35–55 kg)
Gestation: 7+ months
No. of young: 1
Longevity: 10–12 years
Spoor length: 1.5–2 inches (4–5 cm)

Brown with white belly; long-necked; when browsing, often stands on hind legs; diurnal. Remarkable member of the gazelle tribe with uniquely adapted long legs and neck which allow it to reach the upper parts of acacia trees. Usually seen in pairs or small family groups. Restricted to drier parts of Tanzania, Kenya, Somalia and Ethiopia.

Mammal Spoor (Footprints)

Aardvark (Antbear)

Cape Clawless Otter

Cheetah

Genet

Jackal

Leopard

Lion

Mongoose

Spotted Hyena

Wild dog

Buffalo

Elephant

Hippo

Dikdik

Black Rhino

Giraffe

Gazelle/Impala

Reedbuck

Sitatunga

Warthog

Waterbuck/Sable/ Gemsbok

Wildebeest

Zebra

Reptile

ILLUSTRATIONS AND DESCRIPTIONS

Nile Monitor (Leguaan) *(Varanus niloticus)*

Length: 6.5 feet (2+ m)
Weight: 22 pounds (10 kg)
No. of eggs laid: 20–60
Incubation period: 2 months
Longevity: 20 years
A large lizard with a long, slender body and a forked tongue, brown to green in color with black and yellow spots and yellow bands across the tail.

Nile Crocodile *(Crocodylus niloticus)*

Length: 16+ feet (5+ m)
Weight: 2200+ pounds (1000+ kg)
No. of eggs laid: 20–60
Incubation period: 90 days
Longevity: 60+ years
Usually seen basking on sandbanks; often attacks animals walking close to the water's edge from underwater, dragging the prey underwater and drowning it.

Chameleon *(Chamaeleo dilepis)*

Length: 1 foot (30 cm)
Weight: 5 ounces (150 g)
No. of eggs laid: 12–25
Incubation period: 120–140 days
Longevity: 7 years
A slow-moving lizard with the ability to change color and to move each eye independently; catches insects with its long tongue, which can be shot out a distance equivalent to the length of its body; has a prehensile tail.

Python *(Python sebae)*

Length: 20+ feet (6+ m)
Weight: 200 pounds (90 kg)
No. of eggs laid: 30–50
Longevity: 30 years
A non-poisonous but immensely powerful snake with a light-brown skin with black-edged, irregular-shaped dark brown blotches and an elongated spear-shaped head.

Leopard Tortoise *(Geochelone pardalis)*

Length: 12–24 inches (30 to 60 cm)
Weight: 17.5–26.5 pounds (8–12 kg) (exceptionally over 44 pounds [20 kg])
No. of eggs laid: 6–15
Incubation period: 10–15 months
Longevity: 30 years (up to 75 in captivity)
Large tortoise with dome-shaped shell. Moves about slowly in dry savannah and grassland habitats; does not swim but drinks when water is available. Feeds on plant foliage and berries. Ping-pong-ball-shaped eggs are laid in a shallow burrow. Young are vulnerable to predators such as hornbills and hyenas, adults to bush fires.

Agama Lizard *(Agama and Acanthocerus species)*

Length: 3–6 inches (8–16 cm)
No. of eggs laid: 5–14
Incubation period: 90 days
Longevity: 5–6 years
A large-headed lizard, the male has a brightly colored head of blue, orange or pink; female is drab brown. Occurs singly or in pairs on boulders or large trees (depending upon the species). Often bobs head up and down. Not poisonous but able to deliver a serious bite if handled. Feeds on insects which are caught after a short chase.

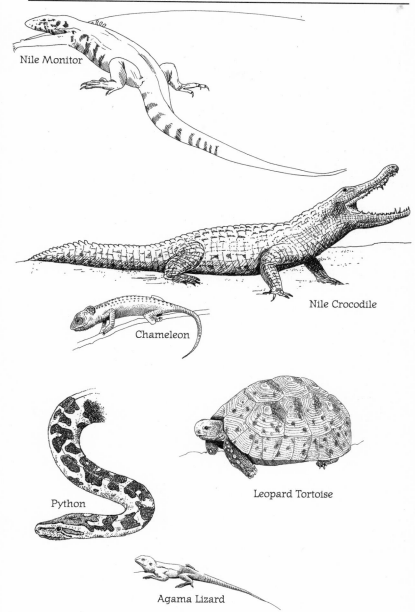

Nile Monitor

Nile Crocodile

Chameleon

Python

Leopard Tortoise

Agama Lizard

Bird Identification and Anatomy

Many birds are quite unmistakable and pose no identification problems, but many more pose a challenge and require closer inspection. All you really have to do is know what to look for when you see a bird and how to use your field guide.

The only equipment that you need in order to watch and identify birds is a decent pair of binoculars (7x minimum, 10x maximum; also invaluable for observing mammals in more detail) and this safari journal and/or a good field guide. You should also have a pencil for making field notes or rough sketches in your journal. It is always a good idea to study this journal and perhaps purchase and study a field guide in advance so that you are familiar with birds you might see before you encounter them! The birds featured in this *African Safari Journal* are among the more common and conspicuous in eastern and southern Africa; they represent most of the families and groupings, so they should be of assistance in pointing you in the right direction.

It is important to remember that you should always closely observe the bird you are looking at (and struggling to identify) for as long as possible before reaching for your journal or field guide. Make a mental note of its distinctive features and then go to the journal or field guide to check them out. This helps to reduce the prospect of seeing features which a bird ought to have, rather than what it really has, by matching it to an illustration. If you're lucky, you'll have the bird in view and the field guide open at the same time.

FAMILY TRAITS

The first thing to do when you see a particular bird is try to put it into a family group. A pelican or owl, for example, poses no problem in this regard, but you will need to familiarize yourself with the characteristics of less distinctive bird families by paging through this book or your chosen field guide. Once you have determined the family, or group, to which a bird belongs, you have already reduced your "options" by a high percentage and are well on the way to making a positive identification.

SIZE

Approximate size is very important in bird identification, but when a bird is alone it is not always easy to judge its size. Try to imagine a species with which you are familiar from your home area perched alongside the one you are looking at. Is it smaller or larger than a sparrow? Is it bigger than a crow?

BEHAVIOR, PLACE AND TIME

Because different groups of birds demonstrate different behaviors, what a bird is doing is often a clue to its identity. Is the bird alone, in a group or in a large flock? Is it capturing small insects in flight, pecking at the ground, drilling into mud at the edge of a pond or flying in a "V" formation? The habitat in which a bird is seen is also of great importance, as is the time of year, because some species are seasonal migrants.

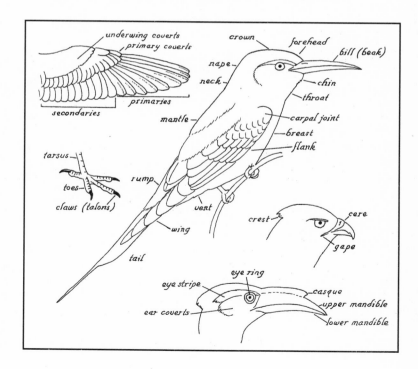

PHYSICAL FEATURES

All bird species have unique physical features and specific or combined field marks (as they are known to bird watchers) which distinguish each kind of bird from the others. With the exception of some warblers, larks and pipits (for which the call or song is vital for accurate identification), the great majority of birds may be identified by their field marks. You need to become familiar with the names of the parts of a bird's body; the diagram on the previous page shows these features. All field guides refer to this terminology.

CALLS

All bird species have unique calls or songs, and regional populations of the same species often exhibit variations. If you are able to recognize birds by their calls, you can record many more species in a given area than if you were relying on sight alone. Hearing an unfamiliar or unrecognizable call will also alert you to the presence of an unusual species and may often allow you to obtain a view.

Many people try to put a name to every bird they see, even if they don't obtain a clear view. This is fine for the birds you are very familiar with, but should not be attempted otherwise. A high percentage of birds are destined to "get away" before they can be identified, and although frustrating, this is very much a part of the thrill of birding. Birds of prey often soar too high for observation with binoculars, wading birds often feed too far away to get a view (even with a spotting scope) and heat haze frequently obscures key field marks. Crakes, flufftails, many warblers and certain bush shrikes are notoriously secretive and hardly ever allow a good view of themselves. So don't get overly frustrated — it is quite possible to enjoy the birds you cannot identify as much as those you can!

Bird
ILLUSTRATIONS AND DESCRIPTIONS
Ostrich *(Struthio camelus)*

Height: up to 8.5 feet (2.6 m)
World's largest bird and unmistakable. Adult male is black
and white, while female and immature are pale brown.
Occurs in pairs or small groups, with season's offspring.
Favors open areas, where it feeds on grass and seeds. Often
associates with antelope. Wary and able to run at great speed.
The call is a deep booming roar.

Kori Bustard *(Ardeotis kori)*

Length: 53 inches (135 cm)
World's heaviest flying bird at 42 pounds (19 kg). Plumage
predominantly fawn and grey; sexes are alike. Favors open
country, where it strides slowly in search of insects, lizards
and seeds. Prior to breeding, the male engages in a dramatic
courtship display which includes the puffing out of the white
neck feathers. The call is a deep, resonant "ooom."

Secretarybird *(Sagittarius serpentarius)*
Length: 55 inches (140 cm)
Unique terrestrial bird of prey with distinctive crest of quill-
like feathers on the back of the head. The bare face is orange
and the legs pink; sexes are alike. Occurs in pairs in open
country, where it searches for snakes, lizards and rodents.
The nest is a large platform of sticks built on the crown of a
flat-topped tree.

African Darter *(Anhinga rufa)*

Length: 31 inches (80 cm)
Dark brown waterbird with long neck — usually held in an "s"
shape — and a long, pointed bill. Breeding adult has a rufous
throat edged in white; sexes are alike. After diving for fish,
the wings are held outstretched to dry. Often seen swimming
with just its head out of the water and then resembles a
snake. Relative of the cormorants.

Reed Cormorant *(Phalacrocorax africanus)*

Length: 20 inches (52 cm)
Black waterbird with long neck, hooked bill and distinctive
red eyes; sexes are alike. Occurs singly or in small groups
along larger rivers and lakes, where it dives for fish. Wings
are held outstretched to dry. Breeds colonially in large trees
or in reed beds, often in the company of egrets or herons.

Greater Flamingo *(Phoenicopterus ruber)*
Length: 56 inches (140 cm)
Tall, slender bird with very long legs and neck. Wings are
rosy-crimson in flight; sexes are alike. Distinguished from the
similar (but smaller) lesser flamingo (the bill of which is a
dark maroon) by its pale pink bill with dark tip. Favors shallow, saline water, often in the company of the lesser flamingo and other wading birds. Feeds on small crustaceans. The
call is a goose-like honk.

Marabou Stork *(Leptoptilos crumeniferus)*
Length: 59 inches (150 cm)
Huge grey and white stork with massive bill and distinctive bare pouch below the throat. The head is bald and the face bare; sexes are alike. Feeds on fish and carrion, often scavenging along with vultures on large carcasses. Usually in small groups, often near camps and towns where refuse is left exposed.

Saddle-Billed Stork
(Ephippiorhynchus senegalensis)
Length: 57 inches (145 cm)
Very tall stork with pied plumage and distinctive red and black bill with yellow "saddle"; sexes are alike, but only the female has yellow eyes. Occurs singly or in pairs on shores of lakes and rivers, where fish and frogs are the main prey. The stick nest is built at the top of a tall tree.

Abdim's (White-Bellied) Stork
(Ciconia abdimii)
Length: 33 inches (85 cm)
Smallish black and white stork with purplish sheen to neck and wings. Blue and red skin encircles the eyes; sexes are alike. Feeds on dry land, with huge flocks sometimes assembling at outbreaks of grasshoppers. Often seen soaring in thermals, sometimes in the company of white storks.

Goliath Heron *(Ardea goliath)*
Length: 55 inches (140 cm)
World's largest heron. The plumage is predominantly grey and rufous, with white throat; sexes are alike. Occurs singly or in pairs, often standing motionless at the water's edge. Large fish and crabs are the main prey, but baby crocodiles are also taken. Nests are well hidden among reeds.

Green-Backed (Striated) Heron
(Butorides striatus)
Length: 16 inches (40 cm)
Small dark heron, with low-slung posture. The back is a dull olive green and the cap black; sexes are alike. The immature bird is heavily streaked and spotted on the wings. Occurs singly in dense cover alongside rivers and streams, where fish and frogs are the main prey. Utters a sharp bark-like call when disturbed.

Cattle Egret *(Bubulcus ibis)*
Length: 21 inches (54 cm)
All-white egret usually seen away from water in the company of buffalo, elephant and other large mammals, which serve to disturb grasshoppers and other insects then snatched up by the egret. When breeding, the crown, mantle and neck are adorned in buffy plumes; sexes are alike. Roosts and breeds colonially in reed beds or trees.

Hamerkop *(Scopus umbretta)*

Length: 22 inches (56 cm)

Plain brown, with distinctive backward-pointing crest and pointed bill, giving the head a hammer-like shape; sexes are alike. Occurs singly or in pairs, rarely in groups. Stands motionless at water's edge, hunting for frogs or fishes. The nest is a huge dome of thatching grass, sticks and mud, constructed in the fork of a large tree.

African Jacana *(Actophilornis africanus)*

Length: 11 inches (28 cm)

Slender rust-red bird with white face and neck and shield of blue skin on forehead; sexes are alike. Extremely long toes enable it to walk on floating vegetation such as water lily pads. Incubation of the eggs is left to the male (most unusual), which also transports chicks under his wings. Feeds on aquatic insects.

Grey Crowned Crane *(Balearica regulorum)*

Length: 41 inches (105 cm)

Tall elegant bird with beautiful head crest of fine golden plumes; sexes are alike. Usually seen in pairs with recent offspring, but may gather in flocks of 100 or more at abundant food sources. Grass, tubers, bulbs, frogs and insects featured in the diet. The call is a loud trumpeting bray.

Sacred Ibis *(Threskiornis aethiopicus)*

Length: 35 inches (90 cm)

The naked black neck and down-curved bill are distinctive; sexes are alike. Tail of the breeding adult is adorned with black plumes. Occurs in small flocks, which forage in shallow water for fishes and frogs. Breeds colonially in reed beds or trees, often in the company of other species. Takes its name from Egyptian mythology.

Hadeda Ibis *(Bostrychia hagedash)*

Length: 30 inches (76 cm)

Heavy-bodied with purple and emerald sheen to otherwise drab plumage; sexes are alike. One of the noisiest African birds; flocks cry and wail when disturbed or as they leave or arrive at nighttime roosts. Usually seen in small groups, foraging under shade of trees in search of worms and insects. A stick nest is built in an evergreen tree.

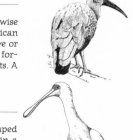

African Spoonbill *(Platalea alba)*

Length: 35 inches (90 cm)

Long-legged, stork-like bird with distinctive spoon-shaped bill; both sexes snow white with pink legs. Bill is used in a sweeping motion to capture small aquatic organisms. Occurs singly or in flocks, which have the habit of flying in "V" formation. Nests in reed beds or in trees.

Egyptian Goose *(Alopochen aegyptiacus)*
Length: 25 inches (65 cm)
Large brown and fawn goose with distinctive white forewings; sexes are alike. Occurs in pairs near water, but may congregate in large flocks when not breeding. Extremely noisy and aggressive, braying loudly and chasing off competitors. Eggs are laid in a large tree hole or in the nest of another bird.

White-Faced Duck *(Dendrocygna viduata)*
Length: 19 inches (48 cm)
Distinctive long-necked duck with an upright posture. The white face, chestnut neck and barred flanks are distinctive; sexes are alike. Often draws attention to itself with its flute-like whistle call. May gather in large flocks at the water's edge. Feeds on aquatic tubers and seeds.

Red-Billed Teal *(Anas erythrorhyncha)*
Length: 18 inches (46 cm)
Distinguished by the combination of red bill and black cap; sexes are alike. Often overlooked as it swims among vegetation along banks of lakes and flooded areas. Often the first duck species to arrive in seasonal floodplains. Feeds on grass seeds, grain and small aquatic creatures. Sometimes gathers in flocks of 1000 or more.

Blacksmith Plover *(Vanellus armatus)*
Length: 12 inches (30 cm)
Conspicuous black, grey and white plover with persistent metallic call (from which it earns its common name); sexes are alike. Usually seen in pairs or family groups in open areas, often devoid of vegetation. May forage on dry land but seldom far from water. Eggs are laid on bare ground, but are wonderfully camouflaged. Feeds on insects.

Crested Francolin *(Francolinus sephaena)*
Length: 14 inches (35 cm)
Boldly marked francolin with distinctive white stripe above the eyes. The bill is grey and the legs pale pink; sexes are alike. Occurs in pairs or family parties, often coming out into the open on sand tracks. Calls loudly at dawn and dusk. Termites and other insects are the main food. Eggs are laid in a ground nest among vegetation.

Helmeted Guineafowl *(Numida meleagris)*
Length: 22 inches (56 cm)
Charcoal grey body is finely spotted in white, and the head is topped with a helmet-like casque. The bare facial skin is sky blue with red forehead and wattles; sexes are alike, but the male has a longer casque. Lives in flocks in dry, open woodland or grasslands. Feeds on insects, often foraging among elephant dung. Call is a repetitive chatter.

White-Backed Vulture *(Gyps africanus)*
Length: 37 inches (95 cm)

Dull brown vulture with long, almost bare neck; the adult becomes paler with age. The distinctive white back of the adult is visible only in flight or when wings are outstretched; sexes are alike. Very gregarious; up to 100 may gather to feed at a large carcass. Dependent upon rising columns of air (thermals) for soaring flight. A single egg is laid in a large stick nest built on a treetop.

Lappet-Faced (Nubian) Vulture
(Torgos tracheliotus)
Length: 39 inches (100 cm)

Huge, impressive vulture, predominantly dark brown and white, with bare red skin on the head and neck; sexes are alike. Dominates other vulture species at carcasses and able to rip open toughest hide with sharp, robust bill. Capable of killing small mammals and birds such as francolin. A single egg is laid in a large platform nest of sticks.

Bateleur *(Terathopius ecaudatus)*
Length: 21–27 inches (55–70 cm)

Stocky eagle with black, chestnut and white plumage. The red skin on the bare face, red legs and extremely short tail are distinctive; sexes are alike. Immature bird is a uniform brown color. The apparent absence of a tail when seen in flight renders it unmistakable. Often seen soaring and gliding low above treetops in open savannah. Captures reptiles, birds and small mammals, but also scavenges alongside vultures.

Martial Eagle *(Polemaetus bellicosus)*
Length: 30–33 inches (78–84 cm)

Huge white-fronted eagle with dark brown head, back and wings. The underbelly is finely spotted and the eyes golden yellow; sexes are alike, but the female is considerably larger. Very powerful predator of game birds, monitor lizards, steenbok and the young of smaller antelope; also takes monkeys, mongooses and warthog piglets.

Tawny Eagle *(Aquila rapax)*
Length: 25–29 inches (65–75 cm)

Variably colored eagle, ranging from dark brown to blonde; sexes are alike, but may belong to different color forms. Bold and dashing predator of birds and mammals, often "pirating" the kills of other birds of prey or storks; may feed on carrion with vultures. Nests on the top of a tall tree; although two eggs are laid, just one nestling survives each season.

African Fish Eagle *(Haliaeetus vocifer)*
Length: 25–29 inches (63–73 cm)

Attractive chestnut and white eagle closely related to the North American bald eagle. The tail is rather short and the bare skin on the face yellow; sexes are alike, but female is larger. Feeds primarily on fish, which are caught in a spectacular surface scoop, but will also scavenge and pirate prey from other birds. The ringing call is one of Africa's most evocative sounds.

251

Lanner Falcon *(Falco biarmicus)*
Length: 16–18 inches (40–45 cm)
Dashing raptor with buffy underparts and silver-grey back and wings; the rufous cap is distinctive. Sexes are alike, but the female is larger. The black streaks below the eyes and pointed wings in flight are typical of falcons. Feeds on doves and other birds, which are captured after a high-speed swoop (falcons are the fastest flying birds).

Yellow-Billed (Black) Kite
(Milvus aegyptius [migrans])
Length: 22 inches (56 cm)
Although plain brown in color, this hawk is easily identified by its deeply forked tail; sexes are alike. Extremely agile; able to twist, turn and feed in mid air. The yellow-billed and black kites are considered distinct species by some authorities. Feeds on small vertebrates but readily scavenges and may be abundant in and around some towns.

Black-Shouldered Kite *(Elanus caeruleus)*
Length: 13 inches (33 cm)
Small, pale grey raptor with white head and underparts and black shoulder patches. The bright red eyes are conspicuous; sexes are alike. The immature bird is blotched and spotted in brown. Feeds mostly on mice, which are pounced upon from a high perch or, more often, from a hovering position. Favors open country with few trees.

Green Pigeon *(Treron calva)*
Length: 12 inches (30 cm)
Colorful but inconspicuous pigeon, with olive to lime green plumage, pale blue eyes and red feet; sexes are alike. Occurs in small flocks, often bursting from cover with noisy wing beats. Feeds primarily on ripe figs, but attracted to other fruit and berries. The call is a distinctive series of clicking notes and whistles.

Emerald-Spotted Dove *(Turtur chalcospilos)*
Length: 8.5 inches (22 cm)
Small, pale grey dove with iridescent green spots on the wings and distinctive chestnut wings when in flight; sexes are alike. The call is a melancholy series of descending notes. Feeds on seeds, often gathering on sand tracks. Occurs singly or in small groups. The small twig nest is sometimes built on an exposed branch.

Brown (Meyer's) Parrot *(Poicephalus meyeri)*
Length: 9 inches (24 cm)
Drab, mostly brown parrot with bright blue rump and yellow shoulders; sexes are alike. Occurs in small flocks which draw attention to themselves by their shrill, piercing calls. Flies speedily with rapid wing beats. Seed pods are the favored food, but soft fruits are also eaten. Eggs are laid in a tree hole cavity.

Purple-Crested Turaco (Lourie)
(Tauraco porphyreolophus)
Length: 18 inches (46 cm)
Spectacular long-tailed bird with crimson wings (seen in flight). The tail and back are deep blue, the underparts green and ochre, and the crest metallic purple; sexes are alike. Occurs in pairs or small flocks in well-wooded habitats, where it feeds on figs and fruit. The call is a harsh "kok-kok-kok." Usually rather shy.

Grey Go-Away Bird (Lourie)
(Corythaixoides concolor)
Length: 18 inches (46 cm)
Pale grey, long-tailed bird with conspicuous crest of lacy feathers; sexes are alike. Very noisy, calling repeatedly "go-away!" from treetops. Occurs in pairs during the breeding season, but large flocks assemble at other times of the year. Most common in dry savannah, but never far from water. Restricted to southern Africa; the similar bare-faced go-away bird is common in East Africa.

Burchell's Coucal *(Centropus burchelli)*
Length: 17 inches (44 cm)
Chestnut-backed bird with black head and creamy white underparts; sexes are alike. Related to true cuckoos, but builds its own nest and raises its own young. Feeds on large insects, frogs and nesting birds. Utters a bubbling call — which sounds like water being poured from a bottle — in early mornings and prior to rain.

Pearl-Spotted Owl *(Glaucidium perlatum)*
Length: 7 inches (18 cm)
Tiny owl with longish tail, often active during daytime. The bright yellow eyes are framed with broad white brows. The call is a whistle, rising to a crescendo and ending in drawn-out notes. Frequently mobbed by other birds when out by day. Feeds on insects, scorpions and small birds. Eggs are laid in a tree hole.

Giant (Verreaux's) Eagle Owl *(Bubo lacteus)*
Length: 25 inches (65 cm)
Huge pale grey owl with black facial rings, dark eyes and distinctive pink eyelids; sexes are alike. Ear tufts give a cat-like profile after dark. Occurs in pairs, often in tall trees along water courses, sometimes in semi-arid scrub land. Preys on birds up to the size of guineafowl and smaller mammals. Eggs are often laid in an old eagle's nest.

Freckled Nightjar *(Caprimulgus tristigma)*
Length: 11 inches (28 cm)
Cryptically plumaged bird; completely nocturnal. A close relative of the North American whippoorwill. Feeds on the wing like a large swallow, capturing small insects with its broad bill. The call is a soft, repetitive dog-like bark. Occurs in the vicinity of rocky outcrops, sometimes perching on sand roads at night.

253

Pied Kingfisher *(Ceryle rudis)*
Length: 11 inches (28 cm)

Conspicuous black and white kingfisher with long black bill. Male differs from female in that it has a double chest bar (she has a single broken bar). Hunts for fish by hovering above water and plunging in after prey. Occurs in pairs or family groups, and lays eggs in a sandbank hole. Often very confiding. Call is a chattering twitter.

Malachite Kingfisher *(Alcedo cristata)*
Length: 5.5 inches (14 cm)

Tiny, jewel-like kingfisher with glittering blue back and long scarlet bill; sexes are alike. The crest is the color of malachite stone, barred black. Perches low among reeds at the water's edge, where tadpoles, small fish and aquatic insects are pursued. Eggs are laid in a sandbank hole. Call is a high-pitched whistle.

Woodland Kingfisher *(Halcyon senegalensis)*
Length: 9 inches (23 cm)

Turquoise-blue kingfisher with black shoulders and red and black bill; sexes are alike. Does not catch fish, but hunts on dry land for lizards and large insects. Favors open areas with tall trees, breeding in tree holes. The call is a piercing, repetitive trill. Populations migrate within the African continent.

Little Bee-Eater *(Merops pusillus)*
Length: 7 inches (17 cm)

Small, green-backed bee-eater with fawn underparts and yellow throat with black collar; sexes are alike. Occurs in pairs or family groups in open woodland, rarely far from water. Captures butterflies and other insects on the wing, usually from a low perch. Roosts at night in reed beds, where many huddle together. Eggs are laid in a burrow.

Carmine Bee-Eater *(Merops nubicoides)*
Length: 14 inches (36 cm)

Large, crimson bee-eater with turquoise cap, rump and vent. A black mask runs through the eye and two long streamers protrude from the tail; sexes are alike. Soars with pointed wings, snapping up grasshoppers, bees and other insects. Breeds in large colonies on sandbanks. Populations migrate within Africa.

Lilac-Breasted Roller *(Coracias caudata)*
Length: 14 inches (36 cm)

Striking, multicolored bird with electric-blue wings and tail; sexes are alike. Streamers protrude beyond the tail. Occurs in pairs in open areas, perching conspicuously on dead trees or termite mounds. Courtship display involves aerial rolls and tumbles. Call is a harsh croak. Eggs are laid in a tree hole.

Ground Hornbill *(Bucorvus leadbeateri)*

Length: 35 inches (90 cm)

Huge, black hornbill with white wing tips. The bare skin on the face is red and the large pick-like bill dark grey; sexes are similar, but the female has a blue patch on her throat. Immature birds are duller. Lives in family groups of up to seven which move in search of snakes, tortoises and other prey. Call is a deep boom. Breeds in a large tree cavity.

Grey Hornbill *(Tockus nasutus)*

Length: 18 inches (46 cm)

Small grey and white hornbill with distinctive white stripe above the eye; male has a casque on a black-tipped bill, while the female has no casque on a red-tipped bill. Occurs in pairs when breeding but may form small flocks at other times. Insects and berries make up the bulk of the diet. The call is a plaintive whistle.

Yellow-Billed Hornbill *(Tockus flavirostris)*

Length: 21.5 inches (55 cm)

Black and white hornbill with distinctive yellow bill; sexes are alike, but female has a noticeably smaller bill. Favors open dry habitats, spending much time on the ground in search of beetles. Nests in a tree cavity, with the female enclosed along with the eggs and undergoing molt during incubation. The call is a hollow "toka-toka-toka."

Black-Collared Barbet *(Lybius torquatus)*

Length: 8 inches (20 cm)

Stocky bird with crimson head bordered by a black collar; sexes are alike. The stout bill is used to excavate tree holes, into which the clutch of eggs is laid. Noisy and conspicuous, it occurs in family groups of three to seven. The call is a loud "du-duddly, du-duddly" duet. Insects, berries and fruit are favored food.

African Hoopoe *(Upupa africana)*

Length: 11 inches (28 cm)

Distinctive brick-red bird with black and white wings and fan-shaped crest. The long curved bill is used for probing the ground for worms and larvae. Usually seen singly or in pairs, most often in open areas. Breeds in a tree cavity, sometimes quite low to the ground. Call is a repetitive "hoop-hoop."

Green (Red-Billed) Woodhoopoe
(Phoeniculus purpureus)

Length: 14 inches (36 cm)

Long-tailed bird with indigo green plumage and striking red bill. Restless and noisy, it occurs in family groups of five to nine. The call is a cackling ramble, made in unison by the group, and often culminating in all birds rocking back and forth on branches. The long, down-curved bill is used to probe bark for larvae. Breeds in a tree hole.

255

Rufous-Naped Lark *(Mirafra africana)*
Length: 7 inches (18 cm)
Drab fawn and brown bird with rufous wings; sexes are alike. A crest of rufous feathers is set on the nape and is raised when the bird is alarmed or calling. Forages and nests on the ground, but perches conspicuously on low bushes and termite mounds. The call is a lovely drawn-out whistle: "tseeu-tseeuoo."

Yellow-Throated Longclaw
(Macronyx croceus)
Length: 8 inches (20 cm)
Drab fawn and brown bird with striking yellow underparts divided by a broad black collar; sexes are alike, but the female is slightly duller. Occurs in pairs in rank grassland or savannah, where it frequently calls with a loud whistle from the tops of shrubs and trees. The nest is a ball of grass. Insects make up the bulk of its diet.

African Pied Wagtail *(Motacilla aguimp)*
Length: 8 inches (20 cm)
Small black and white bird with a long tail that is constantly bobbed up and down; sexes are alike. Occurs in pairs or family groups along rivers and often on lawns at camps and lodges. Small insects and worms are the main food. The nest is built in a rock crevice or under the eaves of a building. Call is a strident whistle.

Black-Eyed (Common) Bulbul
(Pycnonotus barbatus)
Length: 8 inches (20 cm)
Small, drab brown bird with black head and distinctive yellow vent. Occurs in pairs or family groups in well-wooded areas and often tame and confiding at camps. The call is a series of lively whistles, and this is often the first bird to set off the alarm when a snake is present. Small insects and berries are eaten. The nest is a shallow bowl of twigs.

White-Browed (Heuglin's) Robinchat
(Cossypha heuglini)
Length: 8 inches (20 cm)
Striking orange-fronted bird with grey back and bold white stripe above the eyes; sexes are alike. Occurs in pairs, and although typically secretive, it may become confiding in the vicinity of camps and lodges. Extremely vociferous, the call is a strident series of clear whistled notes, usually given at dawn and dusk. Feeds on insects.

Ant-Eating Chat *(Myrmecocichla formicivora)*
Length: 7 inches (18 cm)
Drab, dark brown bird with distinctive white "windows" in the outstretched wings; the male is darker than the female with a small white shoulder patch. Occurs in pairs or family groups in open grassland. Always close to termite mounds, which are used both as perches and underground nest sites. Termites and other insects make up its diet.

Fork-Tailed Drongo *(Dicrurus adsimilis)*
Length: 10 inches (25 cm)

Glossy black bird with distinctive deeply forked tail and dark red eyes; sexes are alike. In flight, the wings are noticeably paler than the body. Occurs singly or in pairs in a variety of habitats, frequently in the company of elephant, giraffe and other large mammals, which attract flies and disturb flying insects which it then snaps up. Call is a jumble of metallic grating notes, but it is also a good mimic of other bird calls.

Common Fiscal *(Lanius collaris)*
Length: 9 inches (23 cm)

Black and white bird with large hooked bill. The long tail and white "v" pattern on the black back are distinctive; female has a rust patch on her flanks. Perches conspicuously in an upright posture on treetops, fences and overhead wires. Feeds mostly on large insects, spearing victims onto thorns for later retrieval. The nest is a small cup, well hidden in foliage. Call is a harsh chatter.

Magpie (Long-Tailed) Shrike
(Corvinella melanoleuca)
Length: 15–20 inches (40–50 cm)

Black bird with extremely long tail and white wing bars; sexes are alike, but female has shorter tail. Occurs in small flocks of up to ten which fly low through open savannah in search of insect prey. Perches conspicuously on top and outer branches of trees. Call is a squeaky whistle: "pruuit-preeuo." The nest is a neat cup of twigs and fibers.

Lesser Striped Swallow *(Hirundo abyssinica)*
Length: 6 inches (15 cm)

Small blue-backed swallow with orange cap and streaked underparts. Occurs in pairs or small flocks, usually near to water. Feeds on the wing, taking small insects such a gnats and fruit flies. Call is a series of nasal mewing notes. The mud pellet nest is built under bridges, rocks or the boughs of large trees. Populations migrate within Africa.

Rattling Cisticola *(Cisticola chiniana)*
Length: 5 inches (13 cm)

Small drab warbler with rufous back streaked in black and pale underparts; sexes are alike. The most common and obvious cisticola in savannah habitats. Noisy and conspicuous, it perches on shrubs and low trees. The call is a distinctive "tchi-tchi-trrrrrrrrr," rattle-like at the end. The nest is a small well-hidden bowl of grass.

Yellow White-Eye *(Zosterops senegalensis)*
Length: 4 inches (11 cm)

Tiny yellow bird with distinctive ring of small white feathers around the eyes; sexes are alike. Occurs in pairs or small flocks which search for aphids and other small insects among leaves. Also eats small berries. Frequently forages in the company of other birds such as warblers, tits and flycatchers. The nest is a neat cup.

Paradise Flycatcher *(Terpsiphone viridis)*
Length: 8 inches (20 cm) (plus 7-inch [18-cm] tail streamers in male)
Beautiful chestnut-backed flycatcher with indigo blue head and grey underparts. The male has a long ribbon-like tail when breeding. Occurs in pairs in well-wooded habitats such as along streams. Feeds on small insects, captured in flight. The call is a warbling "wee-wee-diddly." A tiny egg-cup-sized bowl is the nest.

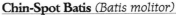

Chin-Spot Batis *(Batis molitor)*
Length: 5 inches (13 cm)
Tiny black and white bird with grey crown and back. Bright yellow eyes are set in a black facial mask. The male has a broad black bar on the breast, while the female has a rufous bar and distinctive spot under the chin. Almost always in pairs, often in the company of other small birds. Call is a three-note whistle: "whi-whi-wheeou."

Scarlet-Chested Sunbird
(Nectarinia senegalensis)

Length: 6 inches (15 cm)
Black bird with thin, down-curved bill and conspicuous scarlet chest patch. The female is dull brown. Feeds on nectar, which is sucked from tube-shaped flowers with the specially adapted bill. Usually seen in pairs, but competing males often chase one another. The nest is a hanging pouch of fiber and spider web, suspended from a branch.

Red-Winged Starling *(Onychognathus morio)*
Length: 10 inches (27 cm)
Large blue-black starling with distinctive rust-red wings most visible in flight; the female is duller with an ashy grey head. Occurs in pairs or small flocks in rocky habitats. The call is a liquid, flute-like whistle. Feeds on berries and insects. The nest is an untidy bowl of grass and fiber.

Superb Starling *(Lamprotornis superbus)*
Length: 8.5 inches (22 cm)
Striking metallic blue starling with orange underparts, pale eye and white on wings; sexes are alike. Occurs in small flocks in open savannah of East Africa, where often common in camps and at picnic sites. Feeds on insects and berries. The call is a harsh chatter. The nest is a clump of straw placed in a tree hole.

Red-Billed Oxpecker
(Buphagus erythrorhynchus)

Length: 8.5 inches (22 cm)
Brown bird with pale underparts and bright red bill. The red eyes are surrounded by yellow skin; sexes are alike. Occurs in small family groups or flocks riding on the backs of giraffe, buffalo and other large mammals. Specialized feeding on ticks, which are combed from the hair of animals with the bill. Call is a scolding "churrr."

White-Headed Buffalo-Weaver
(Dinemellia dinemelli)
Length: 10 inches (25 cm)

White and brown bird with striking scarlet rump, most visible in flight. Occurs in small flocks which feed on the ground in open areas of savannah; present only in East Africa, where often in the company of the superb starling. Feeds on seeds as well as insects. The nest is a loosely woven pouch of straw suspended from a thorn tree, colonial.

Village (Spotted-Backed) Weaver
(Ploceus cucullatus)
Length: 6.5 inches (17 cm)

Bright yellow bird with black mask and black-spotted back; the female is dull and sparrow-like. Occurs in large noisy flocks which breed colonially. The finely woven grass nests are suspended from trees or tall reeds alongside water. Feeds on seeds. The call is a throaty chortle and a series of swizzling notes.

Blue Waxbill *(Uraeginthus angolensis)*
Length: 5 inches (13 cm)

Tiny pale-blue bird with brown back; female has less blue below and is somewhat duller. Occurs in pairs or small flocks, often in the company of other small seed eaters. The red-cheeked cordon-bleu of East Africa differs only in that it has a red cheek patch. The nest is a ball of fine grass stems, often built near a wasp's nest for protection.

Tree
ILLUSTRATIONS AND DESCRIPTIONS

Aloe (*Aloe chabaudii*)
Height: 15–24 inches (40–60 cm)
Medium-size aloe found on lower slopes of hills with granite outcrops; red flowers appear in winter. The bitter-tasting component in the leaf is used cosmetically (aloe vera).

Umbrella Acacia (*Acacia tortilis*)
Height: 50+ feet (15+ m)
The distinct umbrella-shaped tree; well armed with thorns, although the giraffe strips the leaves off the branches with no damage to its tongue.

Baobab (*Adansonia digitata*)
Height: 80+ feet (25+ m)
Its extreme girth (33+ feet/10+ m) and height make it a prominent tree. Flowers in November. Elephants scrape off bark to eat, and baboons eat the cream of tartar seeds from the fruit. Spectacular white flowers open at night and are pollinated by fruit bats.

Ebony Diospyros
(*Diospyros abyssinica*)
Height: 80+ feet (25+ m)
Trunk broken up in rows of rough square blocks; fruit is a yellowy-brown and eaten by birds and mammals. Used to make a very tasty alcoholic beverage.

Lavender Croton (*Croton macrostachys*)
Height: 50+ feet (15+ m)
Fragrant leaves give off a smell when crushed. The leaves are silvery white below. Antelope eat the leaves; birds and squirrels eat the fruit.

Candelabra (*Euphorbia candelabrum*)
Height: 25–50 feet (8–15 m)
Dark green, succulent branches; rhino readily eat the fallen branches. The white sap, which is poisonous and causes blisters when touched, is commonly used to trap fish.

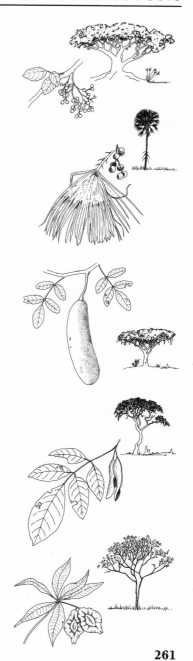

Sycamore Fig
(Ficus sycomorus)
Height: 65 feet (20+ m)
Found along banks of rivers and streams. The uppermost branches are covered by fruit, which is eaten by baboons, monkeys and birds. One species of wasp is responsible for pollinating this tree.

Fan Palm
(Hyphaene petersiana)
Height: 33–50 feet (10–15 m)
Tall palm with hanging fruit. The fronds of young palms form the material for mat and basket weaving. The sap is fermented in the production of an alcoholic beverage.

Sausage Tree
(Kigelia africana)
Height: 65+ feet (20+ m)
Easy to identify by dangling fruit, which is poisonous to humans when unripe. The bell-shaped flowers are sought after by antelope and baboons. Largely pollinated by fruit bats.

Rain Tree
(Lonchocarpus capassa)
Height: 60+ feet (18+ m)
Rather formless tree covered in mauve flowers. During the summer, a group of insects — spittlebugs — live in the tree, and the excess juices they cover themselves with from the tree drip off as "rain."

Silver Terminalia
(Terminalia sericea)
Height: 20–40 feet (6–12 m)
Graceful shape and distinctive silver-grey foliage. The fruit is ringed with a wing and is an attractive dark pink. May form thickets so impenetrable that they exclude other woodland trees.

Mahogany
(Trichilia emetica)
Height: 65+ feet (20+ m)
Covered year round with lush, dark green foliage. Fruit splits open to reveal six red and black seeds, which are eaten by birds, baboons and monkeys.

Savannah Gardenia
(Gardenia volkensii)
Height: 15 feet (5 m)
Small evergreen tree with stiff angular branches and small leathery leaves borne in threes at stem tips. The fragrant white flowers turn yellow with age and are pollinated by a long-snouted moth. The grey, deeply ribbed fruit is eaten by kudu and elephant, which disperse the seeds.

Zambezi Teak
(Baikiaea plurijuga)
Height: 50 feet (15 m)
Tall, well-proportioned tree with dark green compound leaves. Occurs in homogenous stands of tall woodland on deep sand in northern Zimbabwe, Botswana, Zambia and southern Tanzania. The extremely hard and termite-resistant wood is frequently used as timber. The purple flowers are showy but last just a short time. The woody seed pods have a soft velvety skin.

Leadwood Tree
(Combretum imberbe)
Height: 65 feet (20 m)
Tall, deciduous tree with straight trunk and sparse crown. Leaves are small and arranged in pairs on spiny stems. The fruit is a dry four-winged capsule. The bark is pale grey with a rough texture. The wood is hard and very heavy, and the tree is said to live for over 1000 years; even when dead, it remains standing for centuries and is much favored by hole-nesting birds and squirrels.

Checklists

Mammal Checklist
Wildlife Reserve

Mammal	Illustration page number
aardvark (antbear)	225
aardwolf	222
antelope, roan	232
antelope, sable	232
baboon, chacma	218
baboon, olive	
baboon, yellow	
bongo	233
buffalo, Cape	228
bushbaby, greater	218
bushbaby, lesser	219
bushbuck	234
bushpig	230
caracal	220
cat, African wild	220
cat, black-footed	
cheetah	220
chimpanzee	217
civet	221
civet, African palm	
dikdik, Kirk's	237
duiker, blue	
duiker, common or grey	236
duiker, red	236
eland	233
elephant, African	227
fox, bat-eared	223
gazelle, Grant's	239
gazelle, Thomson's	239
gemsbok (oryx)	222
genet, large spotted	221
gerenuk	240
giraffe, Masai	231
giraffe, reticulated	231
giraffe, Rothschild's	231

Mammal Checklist
Wildlife Reserve

								Mammal	Illustration page number
								giraffe, southern	
								gorilla, mountain	217
								grysbok, Sharpe's	237
								hare, scrub	226
								hartebeest, Lichtenstein's	
								hartebeest, red	239
								hedgehog	226
								hippopotamus	228
								hog, giant forest	230
								honey badger (ratel)	224
								hyena, brown	221
								hyena, spotted	221
								hyena, striped	222
								hyrax, rock	228
								hyrax, tree	228
								impala	233
								jackal, black-backed	222
								jackal, golden	222
								jackal, side-striped	223
								klipspringer	238
								kob, Uganda	235
								kudu, greater	233
								kudu, lesser	
								lechwe, red	234
								leopard	219
								lion	219
								meerkat (suricate)	225
								mongoose, banded	224
								mongoose, dwarf	225
								mongoose, marsh	
								mongoose, slender	224
								mongoose, white-tailed	
								mongoose, yellow	
								monkey, colobus, black & white	217

Mammal Checklist
Wildlife Reserve

								Mammal	Illustration page number
								monkey, colobus, red	
								monkey, grey-cheeked mangabey	
								monkey, patas	
								monkey, red-tailed	
								monkey, Syke's	218
								monkey, vervet	218
								nyala	234
								oribi	237
								otter, clawless	223
								pangolin, Temminck's ground	225
								porcupine, African	226
								puku	235
								reedbuck, common	236
								rhino, black	229
								rhino, white	229
								serval	220
								shrew, elephant	
								sitatunga	234
								springbok	239
								springhare	226
								squirrel, ground	227
								squirrel, tree (or Smith's bush)	227
								steenbok	237
								suni	236
								topi	238
								tsessebe	238
								warthog	230
								waterbuck, common	235
								waterbuck, Defassa	235
								wild (hunting) dog	223
								wildebeest, black	
								wildebeest (gnu)	238
								zebra, Burchell's	229
								zebra, Grevy's	229
								zorilla	224

Mammal Checklist
Wildlife Reserve

							Mammal

Reptile Checklist
Wildlife Reserve

								Reptile	Illustration page number
								chameleon	243
								crocodile, Nile	243
								gecko	
								lizard, agama	243
								monitor, Nile (leguaan)	243
								python	243
								skink	
								terrapin	
								toad	
								tortoise, leopard	243

Bird Checklist

Over 265 of the most common and conspicuous birds
likely to be seen in eastern and southern Africa

Wildlife Reserve

								Bird	Illustration page number
								apalis, yellow-breasted	
								avocet	
								babbler, arrow-marked	
								barbet, black-collared	255
								barbet, crested	
								barbet, red and yellow	
								bateleur	251
								batis, chin-spot	258
								bee-eater, blue-cheeked	
								bee-eater, carmine	254
								bee-eater, European	
								bee-eater, little	254
								bee-eater, white-fronted	
								bishop, red	
								bittern, little	
								boubou, slate-colored	
								boubou, tropical	
								brubru	
								bulbul, black-eyed (common)	256
								bunting, cinnamon-breasted rock	
								bunting, golden-breasted	
								bustard, black-bellied	
								bustard, kori	247
								buzzard, augur	
								buzzard, lizard	
								buzzard, steppe	
								canary, yellow-fronted	
								chat, ant-eating	256
								chat, familiar	
								chat, mocking (cliff)	
								chat, sooty	
								chat, stone	
								cisticola, fan-tailed	
								cisticola, rattling	257
								coot, red-knobbed	

Bird Checklist
Wildlife Reserve

							Bird	Illustration page number
							cordon-bleu, red-cheeked	
							cormorant, great (white-breasted)	
							cormorant, reed	247
							coucal, Burchell's	253
							coucal, white-browed	
							courser, two-banded	
							crake, black	
							crane, grey crowned	249
							crane, wattled	
							crombec, long-billed	
							crombec, red-faced	
							crow, pied	
							cuckoo, diederik	
							cuckoo, Klaas's	
							cuckoo, red-breasted	
							cuckoo-shrike, black	
							darter, African	247
							dikkop, water	
							dove, emerald-spotted	252
							dove, laughing	
							dove, Namaqua	
							dove, red-eyed	
							dove, ring-necked	
							drongo, fork-tailed	257
							duck, fulvous	
							duck, knob-billed	
							duck, white-faced	250
							duck, yellow-billed	
							eagle, African fish	251
							eagle, brown snake	
							eagle, crowned	
							eagle, long-crested	
							eagle, martial	251
							eagle, tawny	251

Bird Checklist
Wildlife Reserve

							Bird	Illustration page number
							eagle, Verreaux's (black)	
							eagle, Wahlberg's	
							egret, black	
							egret, cattle	248
							egret, great white	
							egret, little	
							falcon, lanner	252
							falcon, pygmy	
							firefinch, red-billed	
							fiscal, common	257
							fiscal, grey-backed	
							flamingo, greater	247
							flamingo, lesser	
							flycatcher, African blue	
							flycatcher, black	
							flycatcher, paradise	258
							flycatcher, spotted	
							francolin, crested	250
							francolin, red-necked	
							francolin, Swainson's	
							go-away bird, bare-faced	
							go-away bird, grey (lourie)	253
							go-away bird, white-bellied	
							goose, Egyptian	250
							goose, pygmy	
							goose, spur-winged	
							goshawk, dark chanting	
							goshawk, gabar	
							goshawk, little banded (shikra)	
							grebe, little (dabchick)	
							greenshank	
							grenadier, purple	
							guineafowl, crested	
							guineafowl, helmeted	250
							gull, grey-headed	

Bird Checklist
Wildlife Reserve

								Bird	Illustration page number
								gymnogene	
								hamerkop	249
								harrier, African marsh	
								helmetshrike, white	
								heron, black-headed	
								heron, goliath	248
								heron, green-backed	248
								heron, grey	
								heron, purple	
								honeyguide, greater	
								honeyguide, lesser	
								hoopoe, African	255
								hornbill, grey	255
								hornbill, ground	255
								hornbill, red-billed	
								hornbill, silvery-cheeked	
								hornbill, trumpeter	
								hornbill, Von der Decken's	
								hornbill, yellow-billed	255
								ibis, glossy	
								ibis, hadeda	249
								ibis, sacred	249
								jacana, African	249
								kestrel, common (rock)	
								kestrel, lesser	
								kingfisher, giant	
								kingfisher, grey-headed	
								kingfisher, malachite	254
								kingfisher, pied	254
								kingfisher, striped	
								kingfisher, woodland	254
								kite, black-shouldered	252
								kite, yellow-billed (black)	252
								korhaan, red-crested	
								lark, red capped	

Bird Checklist
Wildlife Reserve

Bird	Illustration page number
lark, rufous-naped	256
lark, sabota	
longclaw, rosy-breasted	
longclaw, yellow-throated	256
lovebird, Fischer's	
lovebird, rosy-faced	
mannikin, bronze	
mousebird, blue-naped	
mousebird, red-faced	
mousebird, speckled	
nightjar, fiery-necked	
nightjar, freckled	253
oriole, black-headed	
ostrich	247
owl, African scops	
owl, barn	253
owl, giant (Verreaux's) eagle	
owl, pearl-spotted	
owl, spotted eagle	
oxpecker, red-billed	258
oxpecker, yellow-billed	
parrot, brown (Meyer's)	252
parrot, brown-headed	
parrot, orange-breasted	
pelican, white	
pigeon, green	252
pigeon, olive (rameron)	
pigeon, speckled (rock)	
pipit, grassland (Richard's)	
plover, blacksmith	250
plover, crowned	
plover, Kittlitz's	
plover, three-banded	
prinia, tawny-flanked	
puffback, black-backed	

Bird Checklist
Wildlife Reserve

							Bird	Illustration page number
							pytilia, green-winged (melba finch)	
							quail, common	
							quelea, red-billed	
							robinchat, red-capped (Natal)	
							robinchat, white-browed (Heuglin's)	256
							roller, European	
							roller, lilac-breasted	254
							roller, rufous-crowned (purple)	
							sandgrouse, black-faced	
							sandgrouse, double-banded	
							sandpiper, common	
							sandpiper, wood	
							scimitarbill, common	
							scrubrobin, white-browed	
							secretarybird	247
							shrike, grey-headed bush	
							shrike, magpie (long-tailed)	257
							shrike, red-backed	
							shrike, white-crowned	
							silverbird	
							skimmer, African	
							snipe, painted	
							sparrow, grey-headed	
							sparrow-lark, Fischer's	
							sparrow-weaver, white-browed	
							spoonbill, African	249
							spurfowl, red-necked	
							starling, Burchell's	
							starling, greater blue-eared	
							starling, Hildebrandt's	
							starling, red-winged	258
							starling, Ruppell's long-tailed	
							starling, superb	258
							starling, violet-backed	

Bird Checklist
Wildlife Reserve

								Bird	Illustration page number
								starling, wattled	
								stilt, black-winged	
								stork, Abdim's (white-bellied)	248
								stork, African open-billed	
								stork, European	
								stork, marabou	248
								stork, saddle-billed	248
								stork, yellow-billed	
								sunbird, collared	
								sunbird, scarlet-chested	258
								sunbird, white-bellied	
								swallow, barn (European)	
								swallow, lesser striped	257
								swallow, wire-tailed	
								swift, little	
								swift, palm	
								tchagra, black-crowned	
								teal, Cape	
								teal, red-billed	250
								thrush, kurrichane	
								thrush, spotted morning	
								tinker barbet, yellow-fronted	
								tit, grey penduline	
								tit, southern black	
								tit, white-bellied	
								trogon, narina	
								turaco, purple-crested (lourie)	253
								turaco, Ross's	
								turaco, Schalow's	
								vulture, Egyptian	
								vulture, hooded	
								vulture, lappet-faced (Nubian)	251
								vulture, Ruppell's griffon	
								vulture, white-backed	251
								vulture, white-headed	

Bird Checklist
Wildlife Reserve

Bird	Illustration page number
wagtail, African pied	256
wagtail, yellow	
warbler, grey-backed bleating	
warbler, grey-capped	
warbler, willow	
wattle-eye, common	
waxbill, blue	259
waxbill, common	
weaver, buffalo, red-billed	
weaver, buffalo, white-headed	259
weaver, golden	
weaver, lesser masked	
weaver, red-headed	
weaver, rufous-tailed	
weaver, village (spotted-backed)	259
wheatear, capped	
white-eye, yellow	257
whydah, pin-tailed	
widow, red-collared	
widow, white-winged	
woodhoopoe, green (red-billed)	255
woodpecker, bearded	
woodpecker, cardinal	
woodpecker, Nubian	

Bird Checklist
Wildlife Reserve

						Bird

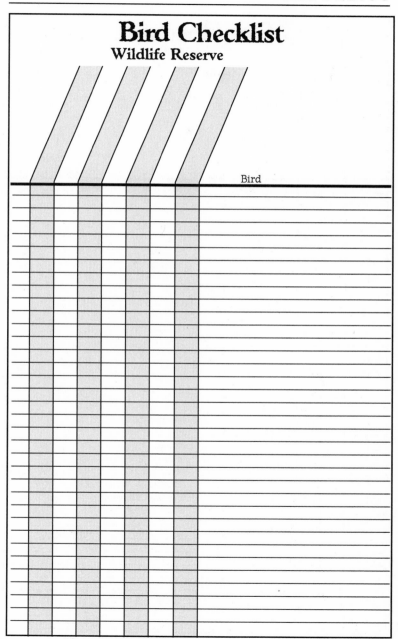

Bird Checklist
Wildlife Reserve

Bird

Tree Checklist
Wildlife Reserve

									Tree	Illustration page number
									acacia, apple ring	
									acacia, stinkbark	
									acacia, umbrella	260
									acacia, yellow-barked (fever tree)	
									aloe	260
									baobab	260
									candelabra	260
									chestnut, African star	
									croton, lavender	260
									date, desert	
									diospyros, ebony	260
									fig, sycamore	261
									gardenia, savannah	262
									leadwood tree	262
									mahogany	262
									mopane	
									msasa	
									palm, fan	261
									palm, wild date	
									rain tree	261
									sausage tree	261
									tamarind	
									teak, Zambezi	262
									terminalia, silver	261
									thorn, wait-a-bit	
									thorn, whistling	

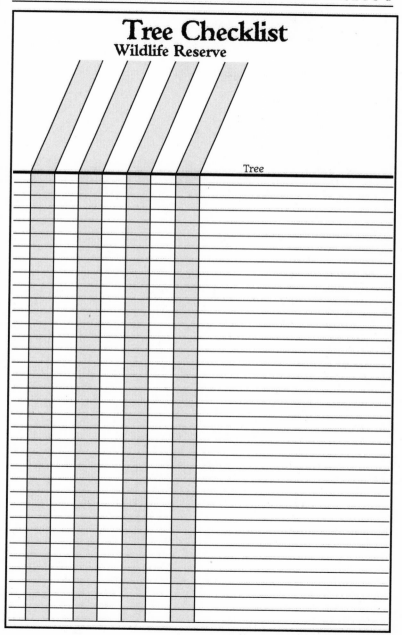

Tree Checklist
Wildlife Reserve

Tree

Other Books from Global Travel Publishers

Africa's Top Wildlife Countries

REVISED FIFTH EDITION

BY MARK NOLTING

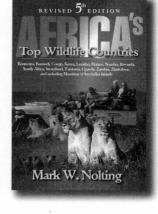

Africa's Top Wildlife Countries highlights and compares wildlife reserves and other major attractions. Makes planning your journey of a lifetime easy! Choose the right time of the year to visit the parks that offer the wildlife and safari activities that interest *you* most!

- Jam-packed with information essential for the successful safari
- Africa's 16 top countries for wildlife
- 53 maps, detailing regions, countries and major wildlife reserves
- 64 color photos, 117 black-and-white photos, 612 pages
- 13 charts, including "When's the Best Time to Go for Game Viewing" and "What Wildlife Is Best Seen Where?"
- Accommodations graded for convenient selection

Global Travel Publishers
P.O. Box 70067
Ft. Lauderdale, FL 33307-0067 USA
Tel: 1-800-882-9453 or 954-491-8877 Fax: 954-491-9060
E-mail: noltingaac@aol.com

What People Are Saying about *Africa's Top Wildlife Countries*

"Nolting does it again! A must for all safari goers traveling in any part of Africa. Along with detailed park information, invaluable safari tips and easy-to-read maps, *Africa's Top Wildlife Countries* is a virtual survival guide that tells travelers everything from what to eat to the best kinds of safaris to what to wear."

R. Michael Wright
President, African Wildlife Foundation

"Faced with the ever-changing scene in Africa, and the increasing variety of options for wildlife trips and safaris, the savviest traveler will reach first for Mark Nolting's *Africa's Top Wildlife Countries*. With detailed descriptions of game reserves and parks in sixteen African countries, plus an extremely useful introduction defining almost twenty types of safaris and safari activities, this book is one of the most practical travel planners on the market."

Ann H. Waigand
Editor, *The Educated Traveler*

"When it comes to Africa trips, Mark Nolting is the man. His book is the first one I reach for."

David Noland
Contributor to *Outside Magazine* and author of *Travels Along the Edge: 40 Ultimate Adventures for the Modern Nomad*

"*Africa's Top Wildlife Countries* is the book to consult for anyone planning an experience of a lifetime in Africa. More than a "must read," Mark Nolting's book has impressive breadth covering game parks in 16 countries in Africa, which enables the reader to make informed choices."

M. T. Hatendi
Zimbabwe Tourist Office-New York

"A unique and splendid piece of work — it tells about wildlife, bird life and the cultural heritage of *Africa's Top Wildlife Countries*."

Edson P. Tembo
Director of North and South America
Zambia National Tourist Board-New York

"*Africa's Top Wildlife Countries* is required reading for anyone with a safari in mind. First of all, it gives a comprehensive picture of wildlife reserves throughout Africa for intelligent, before-you-go planning. It's also a great portable field reference. Finally it is a memory book, even years after your safari — an enduring testament to the wonder that is Africa."

Marie Speed
Editor, *Boca Raton Magazine*

ORDER FORM

Please send me...

_____Copies of *African Safari Journal* @ $16.95 per copy.

_____Copies of *Africa's Top Wildlife Countries* @ $18.95 per copy.

Make checks and money orders payable to Global Travel Publishers, Inc. Mail to Global Travel Publishers, Inc., P.O. Box 70067, Ft. Lauderdale, FL 33307-0067 USA, or call 954-491-8877 or toll-free 1-800-882-9453 (or e-mail: noltingaac@aol.com) and charge to Visa/MasterCard/American Express.

☐ Check/M.O. enclosed

☐ Visa   ☐ MasterCard   ☐ American Express

Card No: _____ Exp: _____

Tel. Day: _____ Home: _____

Signature: _____

Name: _____

Company: _____

Street Address: _____

City: _____ State: _____ Zip: _____

African Safari Journal @ $16.95 per copy................................$ _____

Africa's Top Wildlife Countries, 5ᵀᴴ Edition @ $18.95 per copy ......$ _____

Purchase Total ....$ _____

Sales Tax* ....$ _____

Shipping & Handling** ....$ _____

TOTAL ....$ _____

* Florida residents add 6% sales tax.
** For books shipped within the USA or Canada, add $4.00 for one book and $2.00 for each additional book. For shipping and handling overseas orders, please call for rates.

☐ Please send me your catalog of difficult to find books, maps, audiotapes, binoculars and other safari-related products.

SPECIAL SALES
Discounts for bulk purchases available.

SPECIAL OFFER
Have the name and/or logo of your travel agency, tour company, safari group, organization, etc. gold stamped on the cover!
For details please contact the publisher at
phone: 954-491-8877 or 1-800-882-9453, fax: 954-491-9060